Thomas Hardy's
'Poetical Matter'
Notebook

This book to be destroyed, uncopied, at my death. T.H.

POETICAL MATTER

I

(That has not been experimented on)

[Mostly copied from old notes of many years ago]

Ap.¹ 3. 1873

Titles	The Look of Life / Lines	Poems imaginative & incidental
	Hindsights & other verses	Poems in Sundry shapes
	Souls of men	Souls shown / in verse
	Minutes of years	Poems probably final
	Winter flowers & other verses	Winter Words said in Verse
	Seemings said in verse –	Wintry Things Thought in Verse with other poems.
	A Wintry Voice / in Various Metres Speaks in Verse	

Toll gate. F. Moor. keeper called up : nobody: or enemy
calls him up moment of death. [Cf. "Belle Dame "; "Wife
of Usher's Well " &c.]. Or separated wife calls him periodically:
at last calls; & he will not go down. Her death that night.

— Needles light. (any lighthouse) sitting on the sea. The
sea teazled – Swanage. red-hot cloud. 1876.

The opening page (reduced in size) of the 'Poetical Matter' notebook.

THOMAS HARDY'S 'POETICAL MATTER' NOTEBOOK

Edited by

PAMELA DALZIEL

and

MICHAEL MILLGATE

OXFORD

UNIVERSITY PRESS

OXFORD
UNIVERSITY PRESS

Great Clarendon Street, Oxford OX2 6DP

Oxford University Press is a department of the University of Oxford.
It furthers the University's objective of excellence in research, scholarship,
and education by publishing worldwide in

Oxford New York

Auckland Cape Town Dar es Salaam Hong Kong Karachi
Kuala Lumpur Madrid Melbourne Mexico City Nairobi
New Delhi Shanghai Taipei Toronto

With offices in

Argentina Austria Brazil Chile Czech Republic France Greece
Guatemala Hungary Italy Japan Poland Portugal Singapore
South Korea Switzerland Thailand Turkey Ukraine Vietnam

Oxford is a registered trade mark of Oxford University Press
in the UK and in certain other countries

British Library Cataloguing in Publication Data

Data available

Library of Congress Cataloguing in Publication Data

Data available

Typeset by RefineCatch Limited, Bungay, Suffolk
Printed in Great Britain on acid-free paper by
CPI Antony Rowe Ltd, Wiltshire

ISBN 978–0–19–922849–2

1 3 5 7 9 10 8 6 4 2

Acknowledgements

The editors wish this volume to stand as a special tribute to Bill and Vera Jesty, formerly of Max Gate, whose tireless and richly informed assistance in resolving difficulties of annotation has contributed so much to the completion of this edition, as of so many previous editions of Hardy texts.

Also to be warmly thanked are Marjorie Wynne and Vincent Giroud, formerly of the Beinecke Library; Elizabeth James, of the British Library; and the staffs of the Toronto Reference Library, of the Pratt, Robarts, and Fisher Libraries at the University of Toronto, and of Rare Books and Special Collections and the Koerner Library at the University of British Columbia. Richard Landon, director of the Fisher Library, has been co-operative throughout; Sandra Alston extended her voluntary supervision of the Max Gate Library website to include timely interventions in computer difficulties; Peter Old was both generous and prompt in making available an important item from his Hardy collection; Andrew McNeillie at the Oxford University Press remained sustainingly enthusiastic about the project throughout, and Jacqueline Baker and Fiona Vlemmiks no less sustainingly patient and supportive; while Lilian Swindall, the volunteer effectively in charge of Hardy materials at the Dorset County Museum, was as always wonderfully helpful in devoting so much time and trouble to searching out long lists of sometimes elusive items. Tony Bradbury, Wayne Chose, Ted Clarke, Eleanor Cook, Debra Dearlove, Eva-Marie Kröller, Ann Payne, Michael Rabiger, Dennis Taylor, and Keith Wilson were also most helpful in a variety of ways, and especially to be mentioned among those who have assisted in the search for the original notebook are the late Richard Purdy, the late Frederick B. Adams, Marie-Louise Adams, Daphne Wood, Barbara Jones, Peter Lennon, Ann Soundy, Roger Peers, James E. Gwin, Rosemarie Morgan, Mary Rimmer, and Julie Hetherington.

The editors are above all grateful for the scholarly wisdom of Jane Millgate and the photographic expertise of Bayne Stanley, and for the indispensable patience, support, and practical assistance of both. They also take pleasure in putting on record their appreciation of the generous funding of their work by the Social Sciences and Humanities Research

Council of Canada and their thanks to the Miss Eva Dugdale Will Trust, proprietor of the Hardy copyrights, for permission to edit and publish the 'Poetical Matter I' notebook in its entirety.

Pamela Dalziel
Michael Millgate

Contents

List of Abbreviations

Beinecke	Beinecke Rare Book and Manuscript Library, Yale University
BR	Michael Millgate, *Thomas Hardy: A Biography Revisited* (Oxford: Oxford University Press, 2004)
Bullen	J. B. Bullen, *The Expressive Eye: Fiction and Perception in the Work of Thomas Hardy* (Oxford: Clarendon Press, 1986)
CL	*The Collected Letters of Thomas Hardy*, ed. Richard Little Purdy and Michael Millgate, 7 vols. (Oxford: Clarendon Press, 1978–88)
CPW	*The Complete Poetical Works of Thomas Hardy*, ed. Samuel Hynes, 5 vols. (Oxford: Clarendon Press, 1982–95)
DCM	Dorset County Museum, Dorchester, Dorset
ELH	Emma Lavinia Hardy
Facts	*Thomas Hardy's 'Facts' Notebook: A Critical Edition*, ed. William Greenslade (Aldershot: Ashgate, 2004)
FEH	Florence Emily Hardy
Fisher	Thomas Fisher Rare Book Library, University of Toronto
Hutchins	John Hutchins, *The History and Antiquities of the County of Dorset*, 3rd edn., corrected, augmented, and improved by William Shipp and James Whitworth Hodson, 4 vols. (Westminster: Printed by John Bowyer Nichols and Sons, 1861–73)
LN	*The Literary Notebooks of Thomas Hardy*, ed. Lennart A. Björk, 2 vols. (London: Macmillan, 1985)
LW	Thomas Hardy, *The Life and Work of Thomas Hardy*, ed. Michael Millgate (London: Macmillan, 1984)
OED	*Oxford English Dictionary*
OxfordDNB	*Oxford Dictionary of National Biography*
PN	*The Personal Notebooks of Thomas Hardy*, ed. Richard H. Taylor (London: Macmillan, 1978)

Purdy	Richard Little Purdy, *Thomas Hardy: A Bibliographical Study* (1954; Oxford: at the Clarendon Press, 1968)
PV	*Thomas Hardy's Public Voice: The Essays, Speeches, and Miscellaneous Prose*, ed. Michael Millgate (Oxford: Clarendon Press, 2001)
Studies, Specimens	*Thomas Hardy's 'Studies, Specimens &c.' Notebook*, ed. Pamela Dalziel and Michael Millgate (Oxford: Clarendon Press, 1994)
Taylor, *Language*	Dennis Taylor, *Hardy's Literary Language and Victorian Philology* (Oxford: Clarendon Press, 1993)
Taylor, *Metres*	Dennis Taylor, *Hardy's Metres and Victorian Prosody* (Oxford: Clarendon Press, 1988)
TH	Thomas Hardy
TH Remembered	Martin Ray, *Thomas Hardy Remembered* (Aldershot: Ashgate, 2007)
W	Wessex Edition, i.e., *The Works of Thomas Hardy in Prose and Verse*, 24 vols. (London: Macmillan, 1912–31)

Unless otherwise indicated, all quotations of TH's published verse are from *CPW*, all quotations of his prose fiction from *W*.

Introduction

'Poetical Matter I'—subsequently referred to simply as 'Poetical Matter'—is the last to be published from among the small and correspondingly precious group of notebooks not destroyed by Hardy himself or by his executors. From a biographical standpoint the notebook is perhaps most valuable for its rich expansion and enhancement of what is known about Hardy's final years and its preservation of such remarkable entries as his class-inflected memories of the Bockhampton of his childhood and his sexually charged impressions of a woman glimpsed during a trip on a pleasure steamer in 1868. Its special importance and distinctiveness nevertheless derive from its being, uniquely, an active working notebook, witnessing directly to the persistence of Hardy's extraordinary poetic creativity right up until his death at the age of 87. It demonstrates above all the nature of that creativity, its characteristic progression from idea to completed poem, working with gathered notes, both old and new, through tentative prose formulations and the sketched outlines of possible metres and rhyme schemes, towards the writing of the drafts from which, yet further worked and reworked, a publishable poem might ultimately be derived.

Notebooks were fundamental to Hardy's productivity both as a novelist and as a poet. He had used pocket-sized working notebooks from at least his early twenties onwards, filling them with day-to-day observations on people, places, and things, with stories heard and conversations overheard, with pencil sketches of scenes and situations, and with ideas, images, narrative outlines, and preliminary drafts for possible incorporation into his own prose and verse. Later on, when he was in his mid-seventies, he read systematically through the entire sequence of these pocket-books in preparation for the ghost-writing of *The Life and Work of Thomas Hardy*—the essentially autobiographical work destined to be published after his death and over his wife's name as *The Early Life of Thomas Hardy, 1840–1891* (London: Macmillan, 1928) and *The Later Years of Thomas Hardy, 1892–1928* (London: Macmillan, 1930).[1] Later still he sought to prevent inquisitive scrutiny of his private life and his working methods by personally destroying many such pocket-books and seeking to ensure that the

---

[1] See *LW*, pp. x–xxvii.

remainder would be destroyed by his literary executors immediately after his death. Those precautions were highly effective, and only a few individual leaves from the pocket-books are now in existence, Hardy having detached them for future revisitation, framed them for the sake of pencilled sketches he thought worth preserving, or pasted them into one or other of the more substantial accumulative (sometimes called 'common-place') notebooks that somehow escaped destruction at the time of his death even when bearing, as does 'Poetical Matter' itself, his signed instructions to the contrary.

Two passages in *Life and Work* seem to suggest that at around the turn of the century, prompted by his decision to write no more novels, Hardy may have largely or even entirely abandoned his use of pocket-books.[2] Given, however, the persistence into the later pages of 'Poetical Matter' of references to 'old notes', often dated from within the early years of the twentieth century, and the disappearance and evident destruction of the 'quantities of notes on rhythm and metre: with outlines and experiments in innumerable original measures' described in *Life and Work* as once present among Hardy's papers,[3] it seems clear that Hardy must in any case have continued to make use of notebooks of some kind—one or more of them perhaps devoted specifically to poetry and poetics—that were among those subsequently destroyed.

The notebooks that did survive seem mostly to have done so because Hardy's widow, Florence Emily Hardy, had direct need of their assistance in bringing the 'Life' to a conclusion: the so-called 'Memoranda I' notebook is specifically headed 'This book is to be destroyed when my wife or executors have done using it for extracting any information as to the facts it records, it being left to their judgment if any should be made public. T. H.'[4] It is, however, possible that one or two of the other notebooks—including 'Poetical Matter' itself and the 'Studies, Specimens &c.' notebook mentioned below—were openly or clandestinely preserved by Florence Hardy despite the draconian destructiveness being advocated and pursued by her fellow-executor Sydney Carlyle Cockerell in disregard of the significant discretionary powers assigned to them in Clauses 12 and 13 of Hardy's will.[5]

The accumulative notebooks are clearly of the first importance for the study of Hardy's life and work, and most of them have been in print for

[2] *LW* 328, 346.   [3] *LW* 324.   [4] DCM; transcribed at *PN* 3.
[5] See Michael Millgate, *Testamentary Acts: Browning, Tennyson, James, Hardy* (Oxford: Clarendon Press, 1992), 156–61.

some time: *The Architectural Notebook of Thomas Hardy*, in a photo-facsimile edition prepared and introduced by C. J. P. Beatty (Dorchester: Dorset Natural History and Archaeological Society, 1966; revised edition with enhanced reproductions, 2007); the 'Memoranda I', 'Memoranda II', 'Trumpet-Major', and 'Schools of Painting' notebooks, included with other documentary materials in Richard H. Taylor's edition of *The Personal Notebooks of Thomas Hardy* (London: Macmillan, 1978); 'Literary Notes I', 'Literary Notes II', the so-called '1867' notebook, and the scrapbook headed 'Literary Notes III', collectively edited by Lennart A. Björk in his two-volume *The Literary Notebooks of Thomas Hardy* (London: Macmillan, 1985); *Thomas Hardy's 'Studies, Specimens &c.' Notebook*, a product of Hardy's deliberate self-education as a poet in the 1860s, edited as a type-facsimile by Pamela Dalziel and Michael Millgate (Oxford: Clarendon Press, 1994); and *Thomas Hardy's 'Facts' Notebook*, edited by William Greenslade (Aldershot: Ashgate, 2004) and devoted primarily to items Hardy copied or abstracted from newspapers and other periodicals. 'Poetical Matter', the sole remaining accumulative notebook, has hitherto remained unpublished and rarely examined, even though its exceptional importance was registered in Millgate's *Thomas Hardy: A Biography* (Oxford: Oxford University Press, 1982) and in Dennis Taylor's *Hardy's Literary Language and Victorian Philology* (Oxford: Clarendon Press, 1993).

That 'Poetical Matter' has thus far received little attention is primarily a consequence of the same unusual circumstances as have hindered its publication. When Florence Hardy died in 1937, her will gave directions to her executor, Irene Cooper Willis, for the establishment in the Dorset County Museum (unless Cooper Willis deemed some other museum to be more appropriate) of a Thomas Hardy Memorial Collection that would be kept permanently in a separate room and exclusively dedicated to the housing and exhibition of a collection of Hardy's 'articles manuscripts books and letters' so selected by Cooper Willis herself as to include 'the more important manuscripts and those articles which were most closely associated with my husband or may be regarded as most characteristic of him and his work'.[6] A Hardy Room in the Dorset County Museum was duly opened by John Masefield, then Poet Laureate, in May 1939,[7] but Cooper Willis for some reason delayed in transferring to the Museum the full range of the items she had selected for deposit. The onset of the Second

---

[6] Quoted from Clause 8 of FEH's will; transcription in *Thomas Hardy's Will and Other Wills of His Family* (Mount Durand, Guernsey: Toucan Press, 1967), 6–7.

[7] See Millgate, *Testamentary Acts*, 171–2.

World War imposed still more substantial delays, with the result that when in 1949 Professor Richard Little Purdy of Yale University sought access to source materials essential to the completion of his *Thomas Hardy: A Bibliographical Study* (London: Oxford University Press, 1954), they were still in Cooper Willis's possession. She, however, was sympathetic to his scholarly needs, and in September 1949, during a visit to the United Kingdom, he was allowed to take away—having signed for—several of the most important items not yet delivered to the Dorset County Museum, among them the surviving typescripts of *Early Life* and *Later Years*, the 'Facts' notebook, 'Literary Notes I', 'Literary Notes II', the '1867' notebook, and 'Poetical Matter'.

Three years later, following a request from Cooper Willis for the return of the loaned items, Purdy sent two of the notebooks ('Literary Notes I' and '1867') back from New Haven by registered mail and then—as he told Cooper Willis in a letter of 15 July 1952[8]—packed the remaining items, including 'Poetical Matter', into a 'small carton' that he entrusted to Florence Hardy's nephew Tom Soundy, with whom he was on friendly terms and who was about to return across the Atlantic in his capacity as a wireless officer on the *Queen Elizabeth*. Cooper Willis, though possessed of strong literary interests, was by profession a London solicitor, and it had originally been envisaged that Soundy would simply deliver Purdy's parcel to her chambers in the Temple. In a letter to Purdy of 28 July 1952, however, Cooper Willis reported that she and Soundy had not been able to co-ordinate their arrangements ahead of his ship's departure for New York and that she had therefore asked him to take the parcel for temporary keeping to his aunt Eva Dugdale, who was Florence Hardy's sister and the residuary legatee of her will. She added: 'I am sorry that I cannot check the contents until the beginning of Sept. as I go north on Aug. 1. & cannot fetch the parcel from Miss Dugdale's this week. It will be in safe hands there.'[9] In a further letter of 25 August 1952 she rejected an offer from Purdy (making another of his numerous London visits) to 'fetch the M.S.S. from Miss Dugdale', declaring that she would herself 'fetch them shortly'—even though she had a heavy workload and expected a family emergency to take her out of London again in the immediate future.[10]

Beyond that point the fate of 'Poetical Matter' remains unknown. That

[8] Carbon typescript (Fisher); a complete listing of the items 'Taken by Mr Purdy. Sept. 12. 49' accompanied Cooper Willis's letter to Purdy of 29 Feb. 1952 (Fisher).
[9] Cooper Willis to Purdy, 28 July 1952 (Fisher).
[10] Cooper Willis to Purdy, 25 Aug. 1952 (Fisher).

Tom Soundy delivered the unopened package to his aunt at her west London address there seems no reason to doubt, but how long its contents remained there and under what conditions it is now impossible to tell. It is not even certain that they were comprehensively transferred to Cooper Willis's custody. In July 1959 Cooper Willis assured a scholarly inquirer that 'all notebooks in my possession have been sent to the Museum',[11] and when in September 1962 the final items from the Soundy package (other than 'Poetical Matter') were deposited in the Dorset County Museum, the delivery was recorded in the Museum's archives as having been made jointly by Cooper Willis and Eva Dugdale. The same archives also record that another accumulative item, the 'Literary Notes III' scrapbook, compiled by Hardy but consisting almost entirely of cuttings from newspapers and periodicals, was discovered among Cooper Willis's papers following her death and duly deposited in the Museum in July 1972.[12]

'Poetical Matter', however, is nowhere mentioned in those archives as either an actual or even a prospective acquisition, and since it clearly never arrived at the Museum one can only speculate that it became at some point separated from the other items in the package left with Eva Dugdale and was subsequently lost, stolen, given away, or borrowed and never returned. Just conceivably, its appearance as an exercise book full of miscellaneous pencillings could have led to its being tossed out during zealous housekeeping. In any case, no trace of the manuscript has been turned up by active investigations conducted over the years or by recent public appeals for information. It is of course possible that the original document still somewhere survives, but with the passage of more than fifty years and the intensification of interest in Hardy's poetry it has seemed ever more important—and ever more necessary—to make the contents of 'Poetical Matter' generally accessible by means of a scholarly edition based on the one known and fortunately available witness. Before returning the borrowed Hardy items to England in 1952 Purdy took the precaution of having all of them microfilmed, and it is from the microfilm of 'Poetical Matter' (copies now in the possession of the Beinecke Library and of Michael Millgate) that the present edition has been derived. Microfilm is by no means ideal for editorial purposes, but the legibility of the text has been digitally enhanced, Hardy's hand is rarely problematic, and permission for

---

[11] Cooper Willis to C. J. P. Beatty, 30 July 1959 (Millgate).

[12] Miss Cooper Willis had kindly made this scrapbook available to Michael Millgate when he visited her in 1968, although he felt obliged to decline her further suggestion that he should take it away with him in order to be able to study it further. For the scrapbook itself, see *LN* ii, pp. xxxiii–xxxiv, 253–451.

publication of the edition has been granted by the Trustees of the Miss Eva Dugdale Will Trust, the holder of the remaining Hardy copyrights.

Because 'Poetical Matter' is known to exist only as a microfilm, it is impossible to provide a full description of the copied document itself. Some significant details can, however, be gleaned from that microfilm and from the brief bibliographical description recorded by Richard Purdy while the actual notebook was in his possession. Purdy there describes 'Poetical Matter' as bound in black boards and as bearing both a Max Gate book-label (which would have dated from after Hardy's death) and a bookseller's label indicating its purchase from 'F. G. Longman, Stationer, Dorchester', whose name also appears on other notebooks of Hardy's. Purdy further records that the notebook was wrapped in a paper jacket bearing on the inside a Concord, New Hampshire, postmark, apparently but not certainly dated 28 February 1927 (a time when the notebook was being very actively used), and on the outside front, in red ink, 'This Book to be destroyed, | uncopied, at my death. | T. H.', followed, in green crayon, by 'Poetical Matter | I. | (not experimented on)'. Purdy's additional comment, 'similar heading for 1st page', evidently related to the repetition of the wording but not necessarily to the mode of inscription.

The notebook's leaves, of ruled paper (twenty lines to a page), Purdy specified as being $8 \times 6\frac{1}{4}$ inches in size, written on 'rectos only' and 'almost wholly pencil', but with 'passages erased', some leaves 'partially cut away', and the last third of the book left blank. That Hardy wrote almost exclusively on the rectos is clear from the microfilm, as is the presence of erasures and the excision of segments of several leaves, while the reference to the final blank leaves, considered in relation to the sixty-three text-bearing (though unnumbered) leaves actually reproduced on the microfilm, invites the conclusion that the notebook probably consisted of some one hundred leaves overall. It also appears from the microfilm that the notebook's fore-edge was marbled, as was common with commercial notebooks and ledgers well into the twentieth century. Purdy's phrase 'almost wholly pencil' is somewhat misleading, in that the entries Hardy made directly into the notebook are exclusively in pencil throughout, ink occurring only on the notebook's cover, on its first page (over pencil), and on several of the separate pieces of paper inserted or pasted in at various points.

Hardy's erasures, whether over-written or left as blank spaces, have in several instances (fully indicated in the annotations) been rendered at least partly legible by the microfilm's subjection to current digital processing techniques. That a few over-written words in any case remained minimally legible is evident from the notebook's first page, reproduced as the frontispiece to this edition. The recovery of erased entries, even when only partial, has on several occasions been sufficient to reveal that they had served as the basis for poems subsequently completed by way of one or more separate drafts and included in *Winter Words* (see, e.g., 4.13 and n.). The contents of those segments of individual leaves that Hardy entirely removed cannot of course be reconstructed, but in light of his fear of self-plagiarization—or simply of his need to keep track of his extraordinary poetic activity during his last years—it seems reasonable to assume that the excised passages had also contained ideas, outlines, or even fragmentary drafts for poems he had selected for active development and potential publication. Since all of the excisions occur in the first half of the notebook, it seems possible that they were part of a process by which Hardy, in preparation for *Winter Words*, deliberately cleared away all notes and drafts drawn upon for its predecessor (*Human Shows*), already in the publisher's hands.

Although the purposes and concerns of 'Poetical Matter' are effectively announced in its heading and in the titles for possible poetry volumes inscribed on its first page, it is not altogether easy to determine when Hardy first began to use it. The presence, especially on the notebook's earlier pages, of entries from the working pocket-books—defined by Hardy as 'Mostly copied from old notes of many years ago'—is somewhat reminiscent of the more numerous entries copied into the 'Memoranda I' notebook or, less often, into its successor, 'Memoranda II', both now in the Dorset County Museum and reproduced in *Personal Notebooks*. But while 'Poetical Matter' certainly resembles 'Memoranda I' and 'Memoranda II' in being comprised of ruled sheets and written in pencil, as the other accumulative notebooks are not, it is of larger format than either (both $6\frac{1}{2}$ × 4 inches) and quite distinct in purpose and overall character. Where 'Memoranda I'—essentially a by-product of the preparations for the writing of the autobiographical *Life and Work of Thomas Hardy*—served primarily as a repository of items selectively preserved from Hardy's prose-writing past, and 'Memoranda II' became for the most part a diary-like record of personal events from 1921 onwards that Hardy kept with a view to its being drawn upon by his widow when writing the closing pages of *Life and Work*,[13] 'Poetical Matter' performed an altogether more actively stimulative function in relation to his still ongoing poetic career.

[13] See *LW*, pp. xvi–xviii.

The sequences of 'old notes', often dating back to the nineteenth century, that appear within 'Poetical Matter', especially its earlier pages, seem in any case to have resulted not from any comprehensive review of the pocket-books but from separate and specifically purposive re-examinations probably undertaken once the bulk of *Life and Work* had been completed in late 1920 or early 1921 and Hardy became free to turn his attention back to poetry. Since, for example, the date of 3 April 1873 appearing below the main heading of 'Poetical Matter' clearly relates not to the initiation of the notebook itself but to the specific pocket-book being explored, it is conceivable that the early sequence of Sturminster Newton notes resulted from Hardy's deliberately revisiting the 'happiest time'[14] of his first marriage in the hope of finding it rich in poetic possibilities that might appropriately be captured in what was then an entirely new notebook. As has already been observed, however, the 'old notes' later in 'Poetical Matter' seem to have come from a variety of sources, possibly including a notebook, no longer extant, that was devoted specifically to poetry and poetics.

Although 'Poetical Matter' contains few precise indications of when its entries were being made, it certainly seems significant that neither 'Late Lyrics' nor 'Human Shows' appears in the opening list of potential titles, and that (whatever Hardy's excisions may have contained) none of the notebook's surviving or recoverable notes was developed into a poem included in those volumes. More directly to the point—especially given the evidence from other notebooks that Hardy could be far from prompt in entering material that he had found to be of interest—are such items as the quotation from a 1920 publication, the diagram dated '? 1880–1920', the quotation from a book published in 1923, and the draft poem inscribed on the verso of a form letter dated 29 May 1923 and evidently inserted in the notebook at some subsequent date.[15] Most significant, however, are the November 1927 date on the verso of the 'Woodyates Inn' draft and the cutting from a book review published on 30 October 1926,[16] a date that permits and virtually requires the conclusion that everything in the second half of the notebook was entered during the last fourteen months of Hardy's life. It can therefore with some confidence be proposed that Hardy began using 'Poetical Matter' early in the 1920s and continued to do so, with increased intensity from the autumn of 1926 onwards, until the beginning of his final illness, less than five weeks prior to his death in January 1928.

[14] *LW* 122.   [15] See, respectively, 28.18–29.1 n., 36.4, 71.15–17 n., and 69.2 n.
[16] See 67.1 n. and 36.11 n.

One of the secondary headings of 'Poetical Matter' reads '(That has not been experimented on)', and Hardy, intensely active as a poet until the very day of his death, was correspondingly assiduous in recording materials and ideas in which he perceived some clear or latent promise of creative stimulation or exploitation. In revisiting this 'poetical matter' he marked what he considered particularly promising with a marginal vertical rule or added at the beginning of the note itself a short horizontal rule, a question mark, or his shorthand symbol for 'poem'. That he returned to the notebook's pages on numerous occasions is demonstrated not only by his culling—and frequent erasure—of specific notes eventually developed into *Winter Words* poems but also by his expansions and inter-lineations, as in 'Before it came: bushes grew yellow, sky turned bronze | swart | tan | livid' (19.15–16), and his insertion of supplementary ideas, as in 'Also that makers of things, e.g. painters, writers, builders, furniture makers, are present as ghosts before their works' (15.13–15).

As the notebook progresses, notes presumably copied from the pocket-books increasingly give way to entries of quite a different character, ranging from personal reflections, extracts from books and articles about poetry, and quotations from other poets, to ideas, themes, narrative out-lines, metrical schemes, working notes, and even drafts for individual poems. Particularly remarkable here are the memoranda—'Mth Tender-ness' (36.11), 'Mth. Sting in the tail' (41.11), 'Lyrical Meth' (47.10), 'for process, not for titles' (42.5–6)—that focus on specific poetical methods and effects, and suggest that even during his famous old age Hardy retained something of the autodidactic mode that in the 1860s had characterized his early education as a poet. Similarly unabated was his lifelong fascina-tion with prosodic experimentation: he formulated metrical schemes, considered inverting the third foot in every iambic pentameter line, and linked specific ideas to particular stanza forms such as those in Shelley's 'A widow bird sate mourning for her Love' and Byron's 'Farewell! if ever fondest prayer'. That Hardy was at this period more continuously active as a poet than at almost any other stage of his career is further reflected in the exceptional breadth and character of his reading and thinking, in the reiteration of so many of his defining preoccupations—from satires of circumstance, tragic ballads, and philosophical speculations about 'God', Nature, and Time to experiments with perspective and point of view—and in his constant formulation of entirely new projects, ranging from a verse drama incorporating a chorus of sexually notorious women to a series of lyrics contemplating places only in terms of the emotions they evoked.

'Poetical Matter' also offers rare and sometimes unique insights into Hardy's creative processes as a poet. Responding to a January 1918 query about the composition dates of his poems, he had written: 'Owing to lack of time, through the necessity of novel-writing for magazines, many of the poems were temporarily jotted down to the extent of a stanza or two when the ideas occurred, and put aside till time should serve for finishing them— often not till years after.'[17] The inclusion in 'Poetical Matter' of the detached pocket-book leaves containing draft notes for the never com- pleted 'I sat me down in a foreign town' provides an early example of what such a jotting might consist of: in this instance, a specification of 'ballad metre' for the projected poem, what Hardy himself calls a 'rough outline' of the opening one and a half stanzas, a prose sketch of the narrative plot of the poem as a whole, and an outline of another stanza related to a later point in that plot.[18]

Other 'Poetical Matter' entries show Hardy beginning a poem's devel- opment with notes consisting either of draft fragments of verse or an idea roughed out in prose: 'O Time you frighten me . . .' (26.11) thus became transformed into 'Thoughts at Midnight', while 'The Three Tall Men' had its beginning in 'Melbury man – very tall: made his coffin fearing the car- penter would not make it long enough . . .' (4.13 n.). In such instances as the 'Lady elopes with groom' and 'The Lady who declined' Hardy's initial ideas seem to have been worked up into detailed prose scenarios prior to any verse experimentation;[19] on other occasions the original entry is tran- scribed into the notebook and immediately expanded within a bracketed commentary, as in:

The party at W. P. V. How I slept to the quadrilles – [say on green, outside P. T. Gate: she sleeps – not invited though her lover was: slept all night to the music, as if dancing with him. A happy dream. Discovered next day that he had not come to the party].
                                                                        (37.2–5)

Whatever Hardy's starting point—note, verse fragment, prose scenario, or a combination of these—his customary next stage was evidently the cre- ation of a rough draft (such as those included in 'Poetical Matter' for 'Why should I care' and 'Woodyates Inn'[20]) that would normally be destroyed once he had produced a more finished draft: the rough draft of 'Retty's Phases'[21] appears to be a rare survivor so far as Hardy's almost one thou-

---

[17] TH to Edmund Gosse, 28 Jan. 1918, *CL* v. 246.   [18] See 76.1–79.5.
[19] See 63.3–8 and 74.1–75.16.   [20] See 51.5–53.9 and 67.1–69.1.
[21] Reproduced in Purdy, facing p. 242, and transcribed at *CPW* iii. 316–17.

sand published poems are concerned. The developed draft itself would
then in most cases be revised, re-copied, and re-revised before publication,
often through a sequence of successive drafts, and even published poems
might well be further revised for subsequent editions.

Hardy's poetic creativity was clearly ignited in different ways by the
materials he entered into this last notebook. On the one hand, the fragmen-
tary verse lines which inspired 'Thoughts at Midnight' bear very little
resemblance to the text of the published poem, and what began as an
apostrophe to Time (or Years or Life) becomes an address to Mankind.
On the other hand, identification of the notes developed into 'The Three
Tall Men' or 'In the Marquee' reveals how closely Hardy could adhere to
his original idea. Especially satisfying are the glimpses of Hardy's creati-
vity in 'An Unkindly May', as images and phrases from different 'Poetical
Matter' erasures ('a sour spring day', 'dirty clouds carried lumberingly
along', 'dishevelled vultures – gaunt, shabby', 'buds have tried to open but
have pinched themselves together again', and so forth)[22] are incorporated
virtually unchanged into an arbitrary but entirely appropriate and char-
acteristically Hardyan framework. Such glimpses also prompt an acute
sense of the richness of the material that Hardy did not live to develop
into poems, the unfulfilled promise of such fragments as: 'I will not be
cheered; it seems a faithlessness' (33.10); 'Winter iced the ponds. May
greened the trees' (47.9); and 'What mind, what force, what primary spring
¶ Has cared to do this useless thing?' (66.10–11).

The manuscript's self-identification as 'Poetical Matter I' potentially raises
a question as to whether there might ever have existed another 'Poetical
Matter' notebook, conceivably containing ideas, outlines, or drafts that
had been 'experimented on'. But while Hardy may well from time to time
have had other notebooks that related primarily or even entirely to poetry,
no trace of such a document has ever emerged, and the numbering may
simply have been an act of anticipatory prudence prompted by the exis-
tence of a 'Literary Notes II' and the initiation of a 'Memoranda II'. In
any case—despite Cockerell's comprehensive destruction of what he called
'the first drafts of the poems in Winter Words'[23]—separate and sometimes
multiple manuscripts of *Winter Words* poems derived from the notebook
survive in sufficient numbers to provide a clear indication of the ways in

[22] See 6.8 n., 6.11 n., and 7.1 n.
[23] Cockerell diary entry, 14 Dec. 1928 (British Library), quoted in Millgate, *Testamentary Acts*, 159.

which Hardy was accustomed to move forward beyond the 'Poetical Matter' stage. What ultimately emerges so remarkably from the notebook itself is not only the evidence of Hardy's working methods as a poet but also the astonishing creativity demonstrated by the sheer number of poems thus brought successfully to completion in his last few years and by the profusion of new poetic projects, persistently inventive if often impossibly ambitious, that he continued to propose and contemplate even at the extremities of old age and late career.

Editorial Procedures

As explained in the Introduction, 'Poetical Matter' is known to survive only in a microfilm made for Richard Little Purdy in 1952. Fifty-five years later that microfilm was digitally photographed, and the resulting electronic files processed by Bayne Stanley Photography, the application of unsharp mask and other filters producing admirably crisp images and making possible the recovery of many of Hardy's erasures. The editors have worked closely from this digital text in order to reproduce as closely as practicable the words, spelling, abbreviations, shorthand symbols, pointing, underlining, bracketing, and general layout of Hardy's original. Undeleted alternative readings are recorded as and where they occur in the notebook; struck-through or overscored readings are indicated by a horizontal line drawn through the word or word fragment in question; and Hardy's two substantive slips of the pencil ('growing' for 'going' at 24.5 and 'elewise' for 'elsewise' at 68.18) are left uncorrected. His inconsistencies and pointing errors, mostly failures to close quotation marks or parentheses, are also retained, the only errors corrected being the three instances (at 23.16, 49.9, and 79.10) of redundant full stops. Also omitted are the four instances of 'T.O.' (i.e., 'turn over'), where an entry continues on the next notebook page, specifically at 24.2, following 40.7, at 75.3, and following 80.13. Editorial intrusions in the edited text are limited to the insertion of '*[Excision]*' and '*[Erasure]*' at points where Hardy removed an entry by one of these means, the variation '*[Erasure: largely recovered]*' indicating that most of the erased text is present in the relevant annotation.

Some minor standardizations of layout have, however, been introduced for practical and occasionally aesthetic reasons. The page and line lengths of the original notebook have not been maintained; interlinear additions have been brought into the line; spacing (as between words and lines) has been regularized; and occasional over-writings of individual words (e.g., when Hardy wrote 'he' over 'I' in the ballad narrative at 76.15 ff.) are not shown in the text but are described in the relevant annotation.

The text of the notebook is set in 11-pt type. Typeset notebook entries extracted from periodicals are indicated by the use of 9-pt type. Thus in the following entry the quotation is cut from a periodical, and the date and query are in Hardy's hand:

> 'all the charm of all the Muses   Jan. 1918.
> flowering often in some lonely word.'   Quotation from where?
>
>   (29.3–4)

The edition makes no typographical distinction between pencil and ink inscriptions, but the original is almost entirely in pencil, and all uses of ink (limited to the cover, the heading on the opening page, and several of the inserted pieces of paper) are recorded in the Annotations.

 The Annotations, keyed to the text by page and line numbers, also provide details of all the notebook's excisions—those points at which sections of leaves have been physically removed—and of all the blank spaces created by erasures. Where extensively recoverable, the erased entries are transcribed in the Annotations, angle brackets being employed to acknowledge the tentativeness of particular readings and to indicate the approximate length of the word or words that have eluded recovery, as in 'sun frowns, a <dark > light' (6.11 n.). Erasures subsequently overwritten are acknowledged and, where recoverable, transcribed. The only erasures not recorded are those indicative of second thoughts during the actual process of copying or composition: when, for example, Hardy wrote 'As in "Desperate Remedies" where Cytherea hears sounds', then erased 'sounds', and concluded 'strange sounds, &c –' (42.16–17).

 Hardy's normal practice when entering pocket-book notes into 'Poetical Matter' appears to have been to transcribe the pre-existing notes more or less as they appeared in their original source and then to add identifications, explanations, amplifications, memoranda, queries, or draft phrases, usually within parentheses or square brackets, as in the following examples:

The harmonious munch of cows (in the meadows. S. Newton)   (7.8)

"I don't like to stay here!" Mrs Ashley removes her husband, dead 21 years, from Kensal Green to Stratton. (Mem. "Usher's Well").
[the grave – my cottage, my cellar –]

                        (14.6–9)

A mere question of Time. Man in love with woman who will not notice him: sees that time is injuring her beauty: knows that if he waits she will be his: his nature is a devoted & faithful one. (But how about the chance of her marrying? She may be wife of absent husband perhaps.) Both this & previous poem very short.

                        (19.6–10)

Where the spacing or handwriting indicates that Hardy has added material subsequently to his initial inscription of an entry in 'Poetical Matter'—as, for example, with '[the grave – my cottage, my cellar –]'—

the inserted word or phrase is identified in the Annotations as a late addition. Interlineations are also identified as late additions when editorially judged to be both significant and of late inscription: thus Hardy's extensive elaborations of his note on the thunderstorm at Sandford Orcas at 19.15–20.2 are recorded in the Annotations, but his interlinear insertions of 'a' and 'girl' in 'You do think me a pretty girl' (32.18–33.1) are not.

Unless otherwise indicated, cross-references throughout the edition are always internal, directing attention to another section of the editorial apparatus ('see Introduction'), to specific lines of the edited text ('see 3.7'), or—using 'n.' for 'note'—to a particular annotation ('see 3.7 n.').

Hardy's Shorthand

While Hardy was working as an architect in London in the 1860s, he made several attempts to prepare himself for an alternative career—or combination of careers—that would involve some kind of access to the world of literature and art. His imagination seems not at first to have stretched much beyond such essentially journalistic positions as art critic for a London newspaper or magazine or London correspondent for a provincial newspaper, and it was primarily with such ends in view that he took courses in art history and French and taught himself the shorthand that appears, for example, in the 'Studies, Specimens &c.' notebook and in the margins of a class-book he used when studying French at King's College, London, in 1865.

Among the Hardy papers in the Dorset County Museum is a small bundle of instructional manuals for beginners in shorthand, in one of which, *Taylor's System of Stenography, or Short-hand Writing. . . . Revised and Improved . . . by John Henry Cooke* (London: Simpkin, Marshall, and Co., 1856), Hardy has written: 'T. H. | The best system'. That does indeed appear to have been the system that he adopted, if somewhat freely, and the present editors, when editing 'Studies, Specimens &c.', found that reference to Taylor's manual enabled almost all of Hardy's shorthand to be confidently read. It was, however, more than half a century before Hardy chose to invoke a few shorthand symbols in 'Poetical Matter', and during that period he would seem to have had little or no reason to use or maintain his shorthand skills. While, therefore, the symbols most used in the notebook can again be read with some confidence—as can the handful of shorthand symbols occurring in 'Memoranda II' at a similarly late date (*PN* 59, 100, 101)—they are for the most part adaptations or recollections of Hardy's own past practice rather than precise reproductions of those illustrated in the manual.

However, 'Poetical Matter' also contains two examples, fortunately solitary, of symbols so oddly and perhaps so badly drawn as in one case to make interpretation tentative and in the other to resist interpretation altogether, and the decision has therefore been made to reproduce photographically all symbols appearing in the notebook. The first three below have been interpreted with some degree of confidence; the two others must speak, if at all, for themselves.

Based on Taylor's signs for 'p', 'm', and 's', hence 'poems'.

Taylor's sign for 'p', hence Hardy's abbreviated shorthand symbol for 'poem'. It is found in the notebook's margins or at the beginning of entries and was evidently used to identify material that Hardy considered particularly promising for poetic development.

Within Taylor's system this seems interpretable as 'and so forth', and such a reading would fit well enough with the situations in which it occurs. But since the sign seems more rather than less troublesome than Hardy's customary '&c', it is conceivable that he was using it as an arbitrary symbol of his own, perhaps to register a sense that the idea or topic possessed particular weight or content.

The meaning is unclear, but the crudely represented characters are perhaps intended to represent 'paradox', a concept explored in the immediately following entries.

Indecipherable.

This Book to be destroyed,
uncopied, at my death.
                    T.H.
POETICAL MATTER

I.

(not experimented on)

This book to be destroyed, uncopied, at my death – T.H.

POETICAL MATTER

I

(That has not been experimented on)   5

[Mostly copied from old notes of many years ago –]

Ap.^l 3. 1873

Titles	– The Look of Life	Lives	Poems imaginative & incidental	
	Mindsights & other verses	Poems in Sundry shapes	10
	Souls of men	Souls shown	in verse	
	Minutes of years	Poems probably final	
	Winter flowers & other verses	Winter Words said in Verse.	
	Seemings said in verse –	Wintry Things thought in Verse with other poems.	15

A Wintry Voice | in Various Metres
Speaks in Verse

––––––––––

Toll gate. F. Moor. keeper called up: nobody: or enemy calls him

up moment of death. [Cf. "Belle Dame": "Wife of Usher's Well"   20

&c.]. Or separated wife calls him periodically: at last calls; & he will not go down. Her death that night.

— Needles light – (any lighthouse) sitting on the sea. The sea teazled
   – Swanage – red-hot cloud. 1876.

   Old incapable people – sitting in arm-chair. They see Time
5 pass before their eyes, making no further attempt to plunge
   into it. 1876.

[Erasure]

Late autumn. "A gentle day, when something seems gone from the
garden, & you cannot tell what" (Em.) 1876.

10 Sea-swell against the sun like white satin – detached gusts.

Dead man – the overnight tears of his daughter half-dried upon
his face in the morning. (E. Vincent.)

[Erasure: largely recovered]

Brown dead leaves: the beautiful sunlights they have reflected,
15 &c.   1876

Windy evening at Swanage. The wind shrieks an aria round
angles & posts, & the chimney growls a bass accompaniment   "

A woman. "Eyes of Mediterranean blue" (Em).

Calm day. The air only moving enough to make a faint drone through the crevices of the window. (at Swanage)

(P) *[Excision]*

Rushy Pond in August. To lie among the camomiles, Shep^d's thyme, & wild strawberries. Pigeons come to drink. Almost every bird on the heath has gone afield.   1876   5

———

At S. Newton 1876. Rain, like a banner of gauze waved in folds across the scene.

Clouds of fog like <u>breath</u>: birds ascend through it & sun themselves.   10

At Blandford, 1876. Night on the bridge at the bottom of the town. Light shines from a window across the stream: the surface of the stream seen moving on, the little ripples showing. Occasionally an insect of night touched the water just in the spot   15 of light, & was, unknown to himself, as visible as in day.

No autumn tints, or very brief ones, this year (1876) The frost has come so suddenly that the waiting period of the leaf has been curtailed, so that summer & winter seem to meet on the trees in one night.

5 *[Erasure: largely recovered]*

Sunset through a leafless hedge: the twigs like etchings on a gold plate.

[Erasure: largely recovered]

Woman's face of the proud type: I never see one, even that of a
10 Duchess, which does not bear evidence of some defeat in the past.

[Erasure: largely recovered]

Sunday. Grannys with round spectacles seen reading the lessons for the day. You see them this year, & the next, & the next, & then you see them no more. (1877)

15 Man comes to terrace to see the sun set. (S. Newton)

Faces met: indices of probable length of lives. . . . . . these are

to die at 40, these at 50, &c.   (1877.)

Reeds by the River Stour – dusk: moths fly up when the reeds are

struck: wild clematis: wild hop.

At Bagber. (where Barnes lived): pool: appletrees: remains of   5

garden, &c. all is there except the house.

At a stile near Sturminster N.: tracks: heel-prints: &c.

The harmonious munch of cows (in the meadows. S. Newton)

[Do you remember] On board the Gravesend boat, on the bridge,
                    [your]   [self]
exposed to the wind, the dashing (widow) at 40, who tries to be a   10

young girl: her face florid when we started: now she has become

sallow, except that every scratch, pimple, or blow that has had its

day on her face during the last 20 yrs. & departed, revives like a

ghost, & all show themselves at one time.

At K. a woman lay outside the window at night in the wet grass &   15

heard the man to whom she was engaged make love to another

woman, his mistress.

<u>At Tooting</u>. A pool of water, & beyond it a lamp: drops of rain
cause flashes. (1878)

Going downstairs with taper: its flame reflected in the glass of
each picture, & lighting up the stair-rods.   (1878)

5   <u>Shines</u>. 19 Jan. 1879. In the study firelight a red glow is on the
polished sides & arch of the grate: firebrick back red hot: the
polish of fireirons shines: underside of mantel reddened: also a
shine on the leg of the table, & the ashes under the grate, lit from
above like a torrid clime. Faint daylight of a lilac colour almost
10 powerless in the room. Candle behind a screen is reflected in the
glass of the window, falling whitely on book, & on E's face &
hand, a large shade of her head being on wall & ceiling. Light
shines through the loose hair about her temples, & reaches the
skin as sunlight through a brake.

15 Horse standing by river . . . . A quivering wrinkled horse is
reflected in water.

<u>City scene</u>. Snow & hail: looked forward under a grove of
umbrellas, & saw faces under their shade pushing on through the

weather: hard & square faces, whiskered ones, red ones, anxious ones.

Scene – returning from the Derby. Four men playing cards in a cart, the rain drenching them. (1879).

Sunset. A vast bulb of crimson pulp. (March 2) –

Bock^n. Five sorts of moss on one appletree.

Wet at Weymouth. Dark plaits visible on the comparatively smooth sea.

Sir J. Reynolds' portraits of beauties – faded to a ghastly ashen white.

[Erasure]

"Ld Brougham, in the time of his failing intelligence, frequently told his coachman to drive him to Ld Lyndhurst's, who had long been dead." McCarthy.

At the end of a historical play, the ghosts of the real char^s appear on stage (say Macbeth or R^d III) & avenge themselves – say by burning theatre. They have already destroyed Sh.'s soul.

Two persons. One notices the other's appearance changing [tells him or her: says he feels something] dies: or becomes unconscious merely (Cf. "Belle Dame")

May 9. The gale of last week has blasted the young leaves of trees on the wind side, so that they are brown & shrivelled before they have reached their prime.

Old house at Fordingbridge – the initials of people who have lived in it are cut in the bricks round the front door. Heard landrail or corn-crake 1st time this season. Flowers in bloom, Solomon's seal, lilac, colombine, peony, bankshire roses, larkspur, monkshood, guelder rose, laburnum, broom. (at Miss Jones's, Wimborne). Blue bells, robin hoods (at Mr Chislett's). Mid-spring!   May 12–15. 1882

Windy day – every door wrestling with every doorpost, & every sash with its frame.

1883 –

Saw their backs going down the other side of Stinsf^{d} Hill.

(H. & M^r)

Sunset in Aug, grey cloud in one piece, a hole through . . .

Moon like a gold bill hook, or the nail-paring of a goddess. A

blackbird has eaten nearly a whole pear in garden-path in the

course of the day.

A Satire of Circumstance. Man looking from w$^{\underline{w}}$ of hotel with his   5

bride, that day married. A funeral passes. He turns pale. It is that

of his 1$^{\underline{st}}$ wife, whose death he has heard of, & from whom he is

separated. Having lately been intimate with the present one he

has to-day made her the amende honorable. (Oct 1882.)

Another – Eyers of Blandford – musician – "The Crown" – all   10

pictures are of musicians. He is set on by railways, (he ran 2

coaches to Wimborne when the coaching from Salisbury to Dor.

was stopped by railway, & 1 to Dor. & another to Shaftesbury). He

struggles: fights off poverty, & finally succumbs to a rail$^{\underline{y}}$ coming

through his own town – called "A Battle with Steam".   15

At Dorchester Mary saw men carrying a marble figure like a dead

body into Museum.

Point of View – this mad world.

Tardy leave-taking of autumn foliage (Nov. 16) – clinging to

shades of green, & reluctantly abandoning them for yellow –

Oak full-leaved, of a dirty sap green, hazel but a few shades

removed towards yellow, beech laden with "brown pink" leaves,

5   brambles as rich in deep green as in Aug. (1883) –

Nov. (later). Trees baring. Landscape changes from the beautiful

to the curious, from curves to angles, surfaces to lines. (1883)

Courting from bedroom window to bedroom w^w. Swetman &

Maria Childs – about 1775.

10   The 3 sounds – the eternal purl of the river, the song of the

weavers, the clack of the looms – (House under tree, M.) linen,

tick, dowlass.

Still life scene. Pond by T. Lock's. Pond wrinkled, a cow having
                                                         reflections
just come out: the slow waves <u>bend</u> the inverted ~~figures~~ of the

15   other cows without breaking them. The rich reds & duns are as

full coloured in the reflection as in the reality.   (Dec. 1883).

Highway closely lined with ruts. Each pair of ruts connected with

some family history

Dance of Hailstones in storm.

[Excision]

— The Doctor told the husband of a dying woman that she
would probably not live unless she improved in ½ an hour. The
husband went out, & said, "Come out & tell me how she goes on: 5
I shan't bide in there". He walked up & down beside the stream.
She got better, but he had intended to drown himself if otherwise.
(At P. Hinton: the woman had injured herself reed-drawing –
7 children.) 1884.

===========

[Erasure: largely recovered]   10

===========

End of Sept. Seeds of lime-tree (Two Trees) fly out of the tree
like young birds – supported parachute fashion by the leaf
attached . . . Hedges bent with haws & blackberries (Drong):
acorns crack underfoot as you walk. – The will of Nature towards
perfection. But there is the Canker more or less. All suggests that   15
among the myriad worlds of the Universe there may be some
where the apple has no worm, the sheep no rot. (1884)

Oct 12th '84. At Lambing House – an eft enjoying the last ray or
two of the sun that w$^{\underline{d}}$ be worth having till next April.

Nov. 2. Leaves fall like flocks of birds – no wind. The elms have
gone yellow, the oaks have gone brown, the beeches are red.

5 (1884)

"I don't like to stay here!" Mrs Ashley removes her husband,
dead 21 years, from Kensal Green to Stratton. (Mem. "Usher's
Well").

[the grave – my cottage, my cellar –]

10   Sparks from skid of waggon.

July. A camp at night (Stinsf$^{\underline{d}}$ Hill). Waving flames: sparks going up
& seeming to join the throng of stars: flame flickering on tents like
the opening & shutting of an eye: Voices from nooks in the
darkness – some talking earnestly & low in corners, others loud.

15   Faint sheen from interior of some of the tents. Some round the
camp fire sitting, reclining, standing: shine on faces. The fire
seems the thing alive, the persons being still – Songs, &c – (1885)

A wedding: bride not far from 30 looked 22 young featured &

pink – almost pouty <u>going</u>, on arm of giver-away: 15 yrs older

returning on arm of husband. (Miss Ashley, given away by John

Floyer.) 1885.

The History of a Voice in verse: ditto of a Hand.

A white frost. The grass-blades, candied to stiffness: so that   5
                                              graze
they rustle like shavings at the brush of feet.

Froom Valley. Silent afternoon – gnats. Bell-metal sun – stream

stealing noiselessly on: haze: private conversations audible afar:

the murmur of Lewell Mill below. Sept 1887.

I often think of people as moving under enchantment. or   10

somnambulism.

also: Necromancy – an insight possessed enabling a person to see

the thoughts of others. Also that <u>makers of things</u>, e.g. painters,

writers, builders, furniture makers, are present as ghosts before

their works.   15

Also: a familiar spirit consulted (by the poet, seer, narrator)

The enchantment, mesmerism, or what not, works to make a

person, a people, &c., do one set of things while believing

another.

Souls gliding about in the B. M. They are in a sort of dream,
screened by their bodies somewhat, but imaginable. Dissolution is
gnawing at them all, slightly hampered by renovation. Time, in
the great circle of the library, looking into Space. Coughs floating
5   in the same great vault, mixed with the rustle of book-leaves &
the touches of footsteps on the floor. (9 March 1888.)
[Entered M]. Or souls of the authors – midnight –

Feb 24. 1888.
    A farm of Labourers, as they appeared to me when a child in
10 Martin's time; in <u>pink-& yellow Valentine hues</u>: –
    Susan Sq—, & Newnt (e.g. leaning & singing at harvest-supper)
their simple husbands: Newnt's lovers; Ben B's wife, & her lover, &
her hypocrisy; T. Fuller – the schoolmaster, far above his position
in education, but a drunkard; also wife. the lech—s boy T. M....s.
15 Also Walt, Betsy, & Eliza. The school kept by latter, & their char�s,
sensuous, lewd, & careless, as visible even to me at that time – all
incarnadined by passion & youth – obscuring the wrinkles,
creases, & cracks of life as then lived.

<u>London</u>. Footsteps, cabs, &c, passing our lodgings: every echo, pit-pat, &c. that makes up the general noise has behind it a motive, a prepossession, a hope, an aim, a fixed thought forward; perhaps more – a joy, a sorrow, a love, a revenge.

[Also M]   (end of March 1888.) 5

M. Aurelius <u>screened</u> his wife Faustina, & she was always tender to him in consequence.

<u>The man of large mind</u>, soul, experiences. A personage who speaks or writes as if he had come from a much larger & more brilliant capital than London. He is struck with the narrowness & 10 meanness of the streets, the few languages spoken by the educated, the paltriness of the jewels, the poorness of the literature, the wretchedness of the morals. He may be a god, or angel, come from Heaven.

<u>Tragic drama</u>. Farmer has horse on wh. he wins steeplechases. 15 Backs him heavily for moonlight ride. Horse does not win. Owner at night in stable treats him cruelly. Another man enters, strikes farmer for his cruelty & kills him, leaving him lying dead beside the horse. Man hanged.   (Dec. 1890.)

<u>The amusement of the dead</u> – at our errors, or at our wanting to

live on.   Xmas Day 1890.

   Extraordinary gale & rain. Wind pulls at trees like a termagant

seizing another termagant's hair; whizzes like a relaxing spring,

5 combs the grass violently.   Oct 13. 1891.

Pulling down houses in street. Interiors, paperings, f. p's, &c.

<u>The unknown ancestor.</u> J. A. said that a minute after his mother's

death an expression of another person's face passed over hers,

remaining a minute; then changing to the settled calm of her

10 own countenance. He thought it must have been the look of

some ancestor or relative whom he had never known. (or, it

may have been like that of a portrait he had not been able to

identify).   (1891.)

   [Excision]

15   <u>Lying listening.</u> Dead people in churchyard at the Carol singing

in Church, Christmas Day. or at the service generally.

Samuel Wakely – a great musical soul with limited opportunities.

travels, selling strings, music paper, &c

Sept 13. Shaded lamp looks primrose against the crimson sunset,
striated, as I sit writing in (old) study.   (1893)

"May he kiss me once?" Wife to husb$^{\underline{d}}$ as to a lover, who is
breaking his heart for her. . . . . "May he twice?" &c –   5

 A mere question of Time. Man in love with woman who will
not notice him: sees that time is injuring her beauty: knows that if
he waits she will be his: his nature is a devoted & faithful one.
(But how about the chance of her marrying? She may be wife of
absent husband perhaps.) Both this & previous poem very short.   10

Ten tales (in verse) of one woman. 1 By the young man. 2 By
the middle aged man. Another by old man, another bachelor –
&c. She may be dead – & they by her grave. Or they go home
together, compare letters, word for word, almost, alike, etc.

Thunderstorm coming on – Before it came: bushes grew yellow,   15
sky turned bronze | swart | tan | livid – white bull tossing the
clods against black sky, & roaring. Cream in basket sour. Man
carrying scythe struck dead. The furze was as high as a man on

horseback & there were many snakes. (K. at Sandford, with

additions)   1894.

A person, or family, may be abnormally developed on the

imaginative side. They not only imagine ghosts & personalities in

5   every sound & sight, but converse with them, or about them.

Their belief may be that all the world is so many forms of

thought & emotion, choosing, or compelled to choose, these

infinite varieties of expression. Their attitude imparted by fear of

life.   1895.

10   Poem entitled "What does it mean?" – that of a puzzled,

ignorant, groping creature . . . Or merely question as to a fact, e.g.

And did you tell you had been? &c

Titles. The Lightseekers: The Life-Learners: The Anticipators:

The Wrath-Fleers: The Etherealists: The Ecstatics: The Erratics:

15 The Flutterhearts. The Emotionalists: The Life-Fearers.

The verses alternate: "And did you do so & so?" "Twas I did so &

so". Furniture talks also in this way.

   Or these questions & answers may be to & from Historical

Personages.

The biography of an emotion, idea, aspiration, (as of a person): passed on from one to another as a coin.

Conceive a person absolutely without a will, acting solely by the will of others, or by one external will; with boundless aspirations, nevertheless. (end of 1896) 5

Narrative poem? A man's wife, not heard of for many years, drives up to his door in a carriage; lectures him; dies there & then. The wife he is living with comes in. He tells her they must remarry. She is reluctant. (Has a lover?). Jan. 1897

Another. An outdoor man comes home at night. He is a 10 bachelor at lodgings. Finds his room appropriated by a woman.

To-day – has length, & breadth, & thickness, & colour, & voice, & smell. As soon as it becomes Yesterday it is a thin layer among many layers, without size or colour or smell or voice. Jan '97

I cannot help noticing countenances in objects of scenery. 15 e.g. trees, hills, houses, &c.

Passing Harris's nursery. An old decoration in leaves & flowers withered & brown, calico dirty, in conservatory. "Welcome to

Dorchester" on it.   Feb 20. 1897.

"The Dancing Class." (Miss B's.). The chief char.ᵗ a lonely old

maid or bachelor, who hits on this device for society. She sells

5   baby-linen, cradles, (Mrs B–ng–r), &c.

An address to Fog. "You do great things", &c –

P. Town ch. yd. "Remember us!" . . . . People buried there address

me thus. "We knew Weatherbury", &c –   Jan 31. 1898.

also: All things speak incessantly; will keep on addressing; cannot

10   escape them.   Feb. 13. '98

An inquiry by a yew tree on the meaning of the chiming bells –

(say, new ones hung)

Man, in churchyard, or elsewhere, calls up spirits of local

people, whom nobody else remembers. They might argue that the

15   great are so continually called that they are always alive; but

themselves only now & then. He might have said, "I am a

museum of dead men's souls." When he relinquishes them they

ask him to wake them up again.   Nov 5. 1898

Poem to Nature. "Have you seen Him? How do you struggle

on – ?

Another. N's enquiry. Man's ans. "O Mother I see", &c.

A row of ghosts seen. Oneself at different stages.   5.12.'98

Inquiry, or divination, on what each person met in street   5

is doing. $\left\{\begin{array}{l} \text{He is} \\ \text{You are} \dots \end{array}\right.$ $\left\{\begin{array}{l} \text{He is} \\ \text{You are} \dots \text{ &c} – \end{array}\right.$ Dec. 1898.

   The Hand (short poem) A hand seen lying on a rail, gate, or

what not, by moonlight. The owner not seen.

   Man asleep under sheaves in the heat. Messenger, say a child,

arrives to tell him that his dearly loved wife & child are dead, or   10

that she has eloped. The others (reapers?) watch, & don't wake

him: (end) Dramatic moment. [Has this been written?]

Another. People heard indoors rejoicing at the news that they

have come into a fortune, or that the son is not dead. Somebody

comes up. The news is untrue. Outsiders peep through hole in   15

shutter: what shall they do? when tell?

   The tailor's shop. A man, say curate, is accustomed to go to a tailor's once a week, mostly for some little errand, but really to talk to tailor, his friend, who recites poems, &c. Goes towards the shop one day: shutters up: tailor dead. When the shop is again open curate cannot bring himself to go in, knowing he will not

5 see his friend: still avoids growing: an increasing horror at the thought; though he has business there. At last he does go in, dreading to look across the counter where his friend will be <u>not</u>. Finds his friend's son, smiling & youthful, in his father's place.

(from my exp<u>ce</u> at G. D. & J.)

10 <u>Local Names</u>.

The Yellow Cleft (Yall<u>m</u>): Pale Plain: Pale Plantation (ash in winter): Sighing Hill: Hill of Threatening (Black<u>n</u>). Gap of Surprise (Wynyard's): Holy Spring (Holywell, wh. dried up): Wood of Moans (Banger's): White-eyed, Pale-eyed Hill

15 (Lulworth): Hopeless Lane (Long Ash): Humpbacked Hill (Creech): Dell of no Memories, Dreamless Dell: Black as Rainbarrows: &c –

<u>Historic spot</u>. The visitor sees the ancient: the dweller the modern.

A suffering God: an afflicted God: a self-mortifying God: a self-chastizing, self-chastening God: a self-punishing God (i.e. causing defects & pains in the world, wh. is a manifestation of Himself.

> Feb. 1901.

Ezekiel used the Vision as a mere literary form. Enc. Bib.   5

Every box, drawer, book, lumber-room, full of memories.

A wandering through Wessex, in which are encountered all who have lived there, as a singing crowd. The characters are suggested by marks & remains.   Aug. 1901.

Ballads by the Beldame (Nature). 1st pers. "I do not care what lives   10
I save . . . lose: what virtues I destroy . . . (that is, that poets die,
that worthless beings live, &c –)

Wind; here & there, before universal: in fir-wood, low, then
louder, &c. A sour foggy wind from the sea: chilled cuckoo note:
the wooded landscape gray-green.   April 1902.   15
May weather: late appleblooth red, early white: plum, the white
blooth falling; Sycamores passing from pink ("green ruddy") to
green; leaves overpowering catkins of poplars & birches; cold

wind; the sparrows riding on the boughs, tails blown open like

parasols, feathers ruffled in waves, wistful look as if they wished

they had not begun to build.   1902

Wet night, Grey's Bridge. Road shone up as far as the Bow under

5   the lamps, a chain of light on the road all down the town & across

the moor.   Jan 12. 1904

{ Reminiscences by Destiny }
{ Conversations with God. } It relates how, 1000 years before, It

slowly emerged from unconsciousness of action, & is gradually

10   acquiring perceptions of justice & kindness.   April 1905

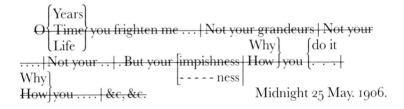

Isochronism. "Accentual [& equal] division of time is the sole

15   source of metre. . . . Accents are major & minor . . . Alliteration

sh$^{\underline{d}}$ probably be on principal accents only . . . Blank verse must

exhibit all the variations of wh. 10 syllables are susceptible . . .

Milton is careful to vary the movement by an occasional inversion of the iambic accentuation: the variation of vowel sounds is also laboriously attended to by him. . . . Variety not for its own sake, but as the emotion varies (?)" <u>Coventry Patmore</u>.

Moon. & clouds. A white smocked shepherd counting his sheep.

———————

"The voice of fear palpitates in [certain spectre ballads]" 5

Ed. Rev^w.

A dread – not of the old spectres, but of those science reveals.

The Persistence, or the Persister – i.e. the Unknowable of Spencer: that which eternally persists = The Will.

An Epic-Drama like "The Dynasts", in which the lapse of 10 time, instead of being within human compass, includes the historic cycles of all the nations from Egypt to England.

Or it might be written as an Epic pure.   29 May 1914.

The "Fly" view of things around. (from old note-book).

"The Ibsen manner: the retrospective manner wh. lets the past 15 facts leak out & accumulate, & then plunges you headlong into the tragic sequel." <u>Times</u>. June 1917

[This is not peculiar to Ibsen]

H. Irving announced to act after death. (See 2 leaves on) Cf. "Wife of U. W." in wh. she keeps wishing her sons w<u>d</u> come.

5   <u>Self "hideously multiplied", or others</u>: or somebody else as wife, sweetheart, husband – e.g. Gen<u>l</u> S. driving up hill, & J.A.)

Or, a driver will not ask a man to ride: finds it is himself many years earlier: at first he does not recognize that it is the same one he keeps passing.

10   Epitaphs.   "So fine a story". <u>Much Ado</u>

"Here must end the story". C. of Errors

"For Remembrance". Hamlet.

"We shall remember". Ant. & Cleo. V.2

"Whose remembrance yet lives." Cym III.1.

15   "No better man". Meas. for M. V.1.

"He doth deserve as much as may be yielded

to a man." Much Ado. III.1. July 1915.

"There are two factors of success in Art, the idea & the

transmission." G. Sampson. [good, but "success" sh^{d} be

"completion."]

      'all the charm of all the Muses   Jan. 1918.

      flowering often in some lonely word.'   Quotation from where?

<h3 style="text-align:center">Addenda.</h3>

In the <u>Times</u> of 14(?) Oct. 1905 the death of Sir Henry Irving

was announced, & on the opposite page was an advertisement

that he w^{d} appear that night in "The Merchant of Venice".

(It will be perceived that the point of this lies in the two

announcements being in the same day's paper – the Times –

14(?) Oct. 1905.)

<u>Henry Irving, to-night</u>, the merchant of venice. Theatre Royal, Bradford.

Next week, Monday and Saturday, the merchant of venice; Tuesday and

Friday, becket; Wednesday, louis xi.; Thursday, king rene's daughter and

the bells. Prince of Wales Theatre, Birmingham.

<u>Sir Henry Irving died suddenly at Bradford last night. He was in his 68th</u>

<u>year.</u> (p. 6)

———

1882. Snow. Its cruelties. "Your cruelties" a poem. e.g.
Hohenlinden, Moscow, Sir J. Franklin, &c. Or, retain the
imagination in one spot, that of the writer?

1883. Sun creeps in-and-in through clothes. Cobwebs glisten,
5   lengthening & shortening their light like elastic needles.

Nov. 9. 1897. Poem. Interrogatories, or Queries, of Fate.

Jan 1899. Poem. "The Sceptic's Doom" He is compelled by his
passion for church music to go continually to Cathedrals &
churches, & sing & sing & sing, unable to leave off. (He may relate
10   this in the manner of The Ancient Mariner)

1907. Dec. 22. Sunday night. Coming back from Bock^{n} in rain.
Ewelease Stile. Ghosts.

1888.   ⅞ Ballads – short – no background:
    "Is there any room at your head?" &c

15   "The time has come $\begin{cases} \text{when} — \smile \\ \text{for} — \smile \end{cases}$ (tune, Allan Water)

Oct 1888. At Evershot Sta^{n} A mistletoe that has been there ever

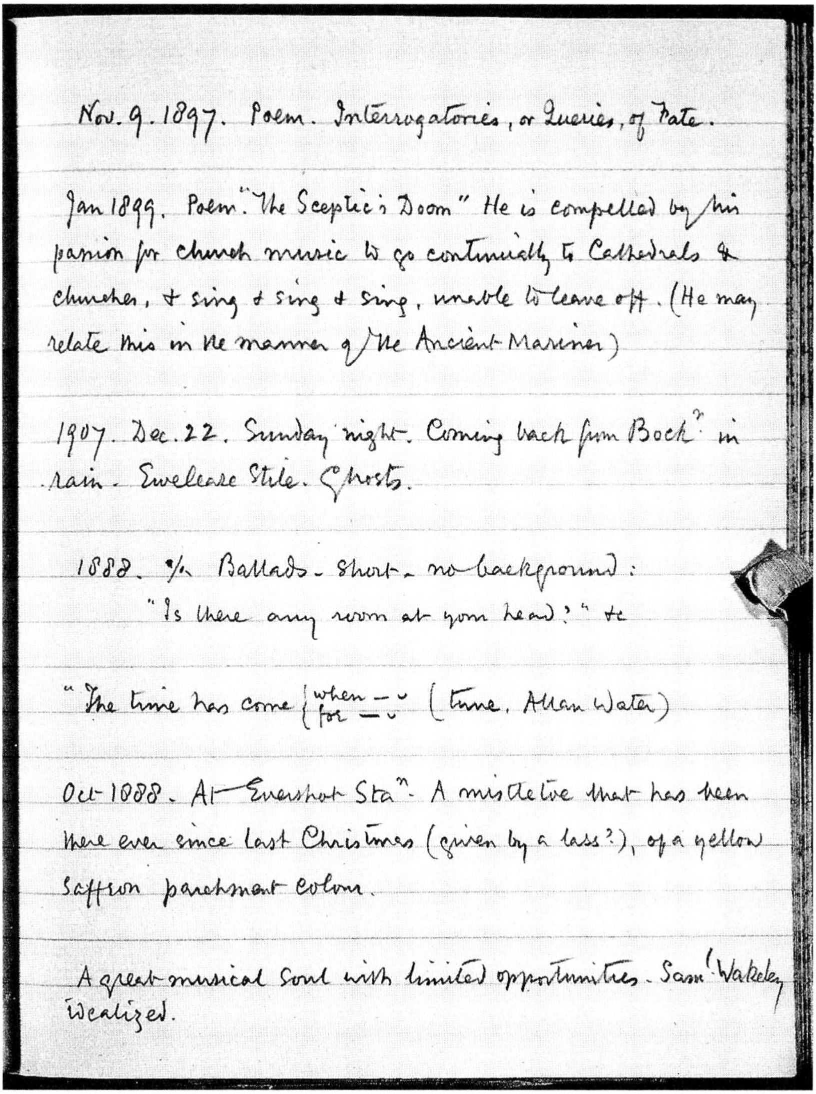

Nov. 9. 1897. Poem. Interrogatories, or Queries, of Fate.

Jan 1899. Poem. "The Sceptic's Doom" He is compelled by his passion for church music to go continually to Cathedrals & churches, + sing & sing & sing, unable to leave off. (He may relate this in the manner of the Ancient Mariner)

1907. Dec. 22. Sunday night. Coming back from Bock? in rain - Sweleare Stile. Ghosts.

1888. 9/. Ballads - Short - no background:
     "Is there any room at your head?" &c

"The time has come { when — ∪ (tune, Allan Water)
                   { for — ∪

Oct 1888. At Evershot Sta". A mistletoe that has been there ever since last Christmas (given by a lass?), of a yellow saffron parchment colour.

A great musical soul with limited opportunities - Sam¹ Wakeley idealized.

Figure 1.

since last Christmas (given by a lass?), of a yellow saffron parchment colour.

A great musical soul with limited opportunities. Saml Wakeley idealized.

[Excision]

1892.

On a Christmas Day: singing in Stinsf^{d} Ch. The three lying listening outside. "They don't do it as we did it in our time." &c.

1894. Scene at Sandford Orcas. Thunderstorm. A white bull tossing the clods against the black sky, & bellowing. The cream in the girl's basket turns sour. A man carrying a scythe was struck dead.

× Woman's beauty fades. Her last sheet anchor, her husband's love, has gone. She gets cosmetics, paint, &c. It is useless. Age continues to claw her. Goes out in the dark, & plays prostitute where her 40 years cannot be seen, where there are tall grenadiers who make love to her. Nobody knows where she has been. The expressed admiration of these lovers solaces her. "You do think

me a pretty girl, don't you? She gets indifferent to her husband's
neglect.

At Harris's (nurseryman) a withered arch-construction of
flowers & leaves – yellow & dusty. "Welcome to Dorchester".

Nov 1. 1898. Bicycled with E. & G. to Black'on Monument.   5
The haunting, insistent, even sinister, figure of the column,
slinking in upon one's glance round as it is approached. Red, dead
ferns – Door prostrate. The weather side crumbling. The howl of
the wind into the top is brought down the staircase.

Dec. 1898. Poem. "I will not be cheered; it seems a faithlessness   10
. . . . . So I will seek the grave . . . . . the old house . . . the ways &
scenes, & inflict blows & weights on me. For what am I, to be
justified in escaping such, as if I were a god, deserving all good?
. . . No," &c (A mean utilitarianism by the very people who frown
virtuously on the utilitarianism of Mill.)   15

————

[Excision]

1872. My. saw a man at P. Hinton come into ch. yard with an

umbrella up. Wandered about in the rain looking for a grave. At
last stopped at old Mayo's. Stood looking fixedly at it: turned to
go: kept his eyes on the grave as he withdrew. Came back again
. . . . . Went on.

5   1872 Nov.ʳ Pallid watery moon. Far away a large white circle.
Moon a greenish light, like that of a druggist's bottle. The large
white ring grows broader, takes away the edge of the moon, &
makes her nebulous.

[Erasure]

10   A young woman, after her marriage, or <u>at the wedding</u>, when
she saw her husband's brother [come to be best man?], said,
"How I wish I had married <u>him</u>!" She used to tell this, saying,
"What do you think of my wicked thoughts!" (Ballad.)

Aug 26. 1868. To Weymouth with Mary. Found it was Wᵗʰ Races.
15   To Lulworth by steamboat. A woman on the paddle-box steps: all
laughter: then part illness & the remainder laughter. M. & I
alighted at Lulᵗʰ Cove: she did not, but went back to Weyᵗʰ with
the steamer. Saw her for the last time standing on deck as the boat
moved off. White feather in hat, brown dress, Dorset dialect,

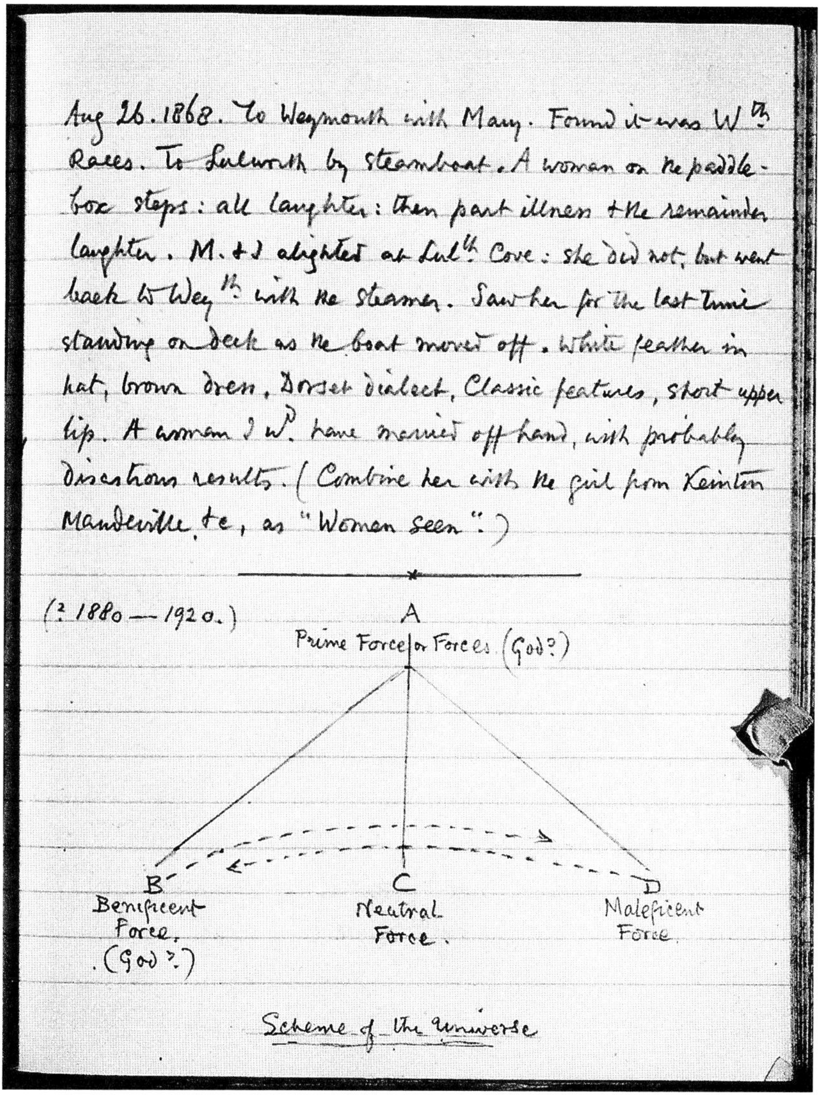

Aug 26. 1868. To Weymouth with Mary. Found it was W[th]
Races. To Lulworth by steamboat. A woman on the paddle-
box steps: all laughter: then part illness + the remainder
laughter. M. + I alighted at Lul[th] Cove: she did not, but went
back to Wey[th] with the steamer. Saw her for the last time
standing on deck as the boat moved off. White feather in
hat, brown dress, Dorset dialect, Classic features, short upper
lip. A woman I w[d]. have married off hand, with probably
disastrous results. (Combine her with the girl from Keinton
Mandeville, &c, as "Women seen".)

(? 1880 — 1920.)

A
Prime Force or Forces (God?)

B
Beneficent
Force.
(God?)

C
Neutral
Force.

D
Maleficent
Force.

Scheme of the universe

Figure 2.

Classic features, short upper lip. A woman I w$^{\underline{d}}$ have married off

hand, with probably disastrous results. (Combine her with the girl

from Keinton Mandeville, &c, as "Women seen".)

———————×———————

5   (? 1880–1920.)

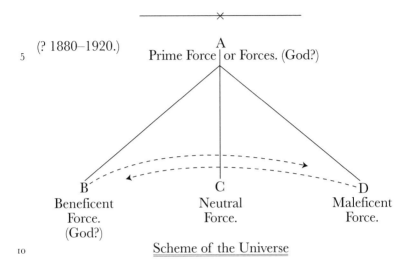

Scheme of the Universe

Mth   Tenderness – (supreme quality)

═══════════════════════════════

A Poetry Book – "Time & Chance". by Mary S. Edwards – Pref.

by Gilbert Murray. Passage quoted by The Nation.

"I know the place, a tree lying

15   Fallen across the pool,

And the little patch of grass drying

Where you left your milking-stool,

And I found you in the dark crying

And kissed you like a fool—"

[Excision]

— The party at W. P. V. How I slept to the quadrilles – [say on
green, outside P. T. Gate: she sleeps not invited though her lover
was: slept all night to the music, as if dancing with him. A happy
dream. Discovered next day that he had not come to the party]   5

— Cerne Abbey. The four apostate monks John Milton, John
London, Philip Shirborn & John Long, who had left the convent
at the election as abbot of John Godmanston 23 July 1436
[because he was unworthy?] – Hutch. IV. 23

— A man goes among people who see him as a ghost, though he   10
does not himself know that he has died & is one.

━━━━━

"There is nae Covenant noo, lassie,

There is nae Covenant noo;

The Solemn League & Covenant

Are a' broken through."   Old Scotch song.   15

━━━━━

ʃ Verse one: Did you not hear? Verse two: Did you not see?

[Erasure]

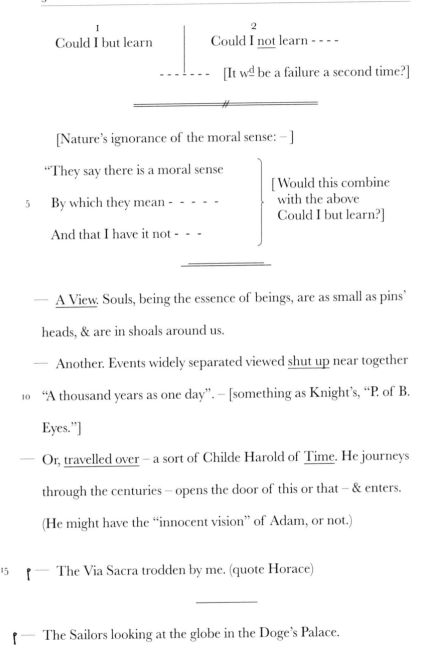

      1
Could I but learn | 2
                 Could I <u>not</u> learn - - - -

- - - - - - - [It w^d be a failure a second time?]

[Nature's ignorance of the moral sense: –]

"They say there is a moral sense

5   By which they mean - - - - -

And that I have it not - - -

[Would this combine
with the above
Could I but learn?]

— <u>A View</u>. Souls, being the essence of beings, are as small as pins'
heads, & are in shoals around us.

— Another. Events widely separated viewed <u>shut up</u> near together

10 "A thousand years as one day". – [something as Knight's, "P. of B.
Eyes."]

— Or, <u>travelled over</u> – a sort of Childe Harold of <u>Time</u>. He journeys
through the centuries – opens the door of this or that – & enters.
(He might have the "innocent vision" of Adam, or not.)

15 ¶ — The Via Sacra trodden by me. (quote Horace)

¶ — The Sailors looking at the globe in the Doge's Palace.

Opening the case containing the Venus: straw, nails, &c.

———————

A room as viewed by a mouse from a chink under skirting: or

a person by a fly: or householders by bird in nest – "They do not

see me".

———————

[Excision]   5

— Why Orion, Pleiades, stars generally, & the Moon are of

interest & beauty.   Not for their size, brightness, distance,

grandeur, &c. but _____ Because on just such an evening, . . .

night . . . Shelley, Wordsw<u>th</u>, Shakesp., Milton, Virgil, Homer

Paul of Tarsus, Jesus of Nazareth, Authors of Job, the Psalms,   10

&c., & all of that brotherhood, have mused on them as I do now.

———————

Ghosts at old Mad House, Forston. The melancholy avenue –

Each tells what he was confined for.

———————

Series of Ghost Poems.

Thoughts, Memories, Fancies, &c, are the Ghosts. (A method   15

of restoring ghost literature) Title might be – "Phantoms not supernatural."

Cerne Abbey.

ʔ   Old houses at Cerne built of fragments of Abbey. Ghosts appear to occupant of a house, asking why, &c. & telling what

5   part of Abbey is in his wall. Or these ghosts are seen, not by author, but by "Men Met" (like Ancient M^r)

ʔ   "The Four Apostates" (monks) v. Hutchins – "Cerne".

Cerne Abbey cont^d

ʔ   Give names of Abbots, monks, & great personages, who are

10   now kicked about by the cows in the Abbey field – "This clod was William Beyminster" – "I am W. B", &c.

ʔ   After looking at the ruins of Cerne, & raising a vision of its prime, & the fervour which led to it: –

Some new { fervour / enthusiasm is now required to produce such

15   another effort –

------------//------------

"God" poem, or poems: – or <u>hymns</u>.

—   Not asking help, but sympathizing with G. – the pathos of nature – in her strivings &c (partly written already)

— God deplores that men invent excuses for him, when he is

inexcusably to blame. (He chose to │ work weave <u>unconsciously</u>, &c)

— God suffers from self-inflicted wounds (Hartm<u>n</u> II. 366 –

Cf. Spinoza, where God is Nature) [continued later, p . . . .]

———————

<u>Time's</u> reflections (as an individual) – I see my ghostly length   5

stretching back like a serpent, or like a river: here rubbing &

seething, there calm; here red with wrath, there pale, cold. Many

a good cause have I stifled, many a vessel of hope has gone down

in me. He goes on to tell what he said & did with various human

beings.   10

<u>Mth.</u> <u>Sting in the tail – descriptive up to then</u> – ♪———

from "Penelope": —   by R. Buchanan.

My very heart has grown a timid mouse

Peeping out, fearful, when the house is still

Breathless I listen thro' the breathless dark,   15

And hear the cock counting the leaden hours,

And in the pauses of his cry, the deep

Swings on the flat sand with a hollow clang;

> And pale and burning-eyed, I fall asleep
>
> When, with wild hair, across the weary wave
>
> Stares the sick Dawn that brings thee not to me.

♪—— "How it was" versus "How it seemed"

5   or "What I saw & what I felt"   (for process,
                                                            not for
     or "Seeing & Thinking" – "Seen & Felt"   titles)

     or "Backgrounds & Foregrounds".

   Thus: give an impression picture of the scene – then an

allusion to some event (connected or mingling with scene?), which

10   is the dominating thought, despite such scene's intrinsic qualities.

(from notes of about 1900)

(Compare the above with "What is it to <u>me</u>?" – & with

Schleirmacher's "The entire outside world is only the stuff for

symbolism" – applying these last to the background-&-

15   foreground idea.)

   As in "Desperate Remedies" where Cytherea hears strange

sounds, &c –

♪—— written on the imagined causes of <u>sounds</u>, <u>sights</u>, <u>smells</u> heard,

seen, &c. high up in an attic in a city, or tower.

Tit. Songs / Poems } of Ignorance. (Cf. Blake)

———

— A poem of little children with matured faces.

— A poem on a dinner-table (Gr—y's old one)

   . . . . on a card table – (the table loq.)

———

Sudden leaps of thought – e.g. "Marie Hamilton's to the kirk   5

gane | Wi' ribbons in her hair | The King thought mair of Marie

H. | Than ony that were there.

———

Scenes requiring keys. "M. Fernand Khnopff's mystical art –

A lady gazing at a mask – her secret," &c –   Academy

From a very old note: about 1905 –   10

Volume of Poems – "Situations" – i.e. two or more people

standing in a scene of their lives, & uttering, motionless, the

emotional dialogue dictated by the position. Tit. "Crises", or

Conjunctures".

— Or, Terrible Tragedies, hinted brokenly, briefly, reluctantly.   15

[✻ see on back]

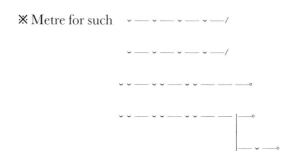

5

‖ A series of poems – When: Who: What.

‖ A <u>moment</u> in the middle of a dramatic story, for poem. i.e.,

whittle down a subject to a mere moment of it.

———————

‖ A mental refrain = refrain of idea, not a verbal repetition

———————

10 He carries fiddle or bass viol to bed for carol. (old man or boy)

———————

Lyrics without chronological sequence – an action being

continuously contemplated without reference to the order of its

details in time

<u>Place</u> lyrics – i.e., contemplate any house, village, town, or

15 what not, in respect <u>only</u> of the emotion it recalls. e.g.

Sturminster, Wimborne, Boscastle, Enfield, Earl's Court Exh[n].

‖ It must be a place which <u>has</u> an emotion.

———

Monologue of the 2$\underline{d}$ wife of the E. of Bristol, who would not have her effigy placed on her husband's left side.

———

A poem beginning "We dug & dug" – which I partly wrote years ago, & cannot find. What was it?   5

——//——

[Excision]

<u>Poem</u>. She is no more met here –

<u>Another</u>. "Before we knew . . . ¶ The — was bright with . . . . ¶ Before we knew, &c

———

Ballads – Thought out first in D. Dialect?   10

———

Short ♪——— Incidents (of 1862–7, 1872, say) on going out, starting in winter, or summer &c – in form, say, of S's Widow Bird.

———

The New View – as I have tried to express it lately in "Shut out

that Moon". A	Whom I have loved Fortune loved not;
	Whom I remember are forgot,
good example	- - - - - - - - - - - - -
	My saints have on the earth no shrine
of it is the	- - - - - - - - - - -
	My prophets none did heed or trust
5 annexed poem.	My conquerors, conquered, bit the dust. &c
	Edith Thomas in The Century Feb '05

[a note copied

from one made

in 1905]

Songs of Things left to be divined. Poems of Tragedies

10 unexplained. Poems of Reticence. Songs of the Half-hidden.

(Songs of the Tragedy beheld in the mind's eye, half-revealed

unconsciously, but not explained) [This idea, written in 1905,

anticipates the modern fashion of poems.] – Also, after reading

some of Sh—y's "Fragments – Short poems of the emotions

15 arising from situations adumbrated but unexplained.

———————

Poetry of the Microscope – in which minute things are regarded

as vast. e.g., on wrinkles, the crow's foot of an eye, the greying of

a hair, the pitting of a neck, wrinkles on back of hand. It might

be in the form of conversations with these. Also with Strength,

| Eyes, Years, Hairs, Heart, Will, Brain, &c. (H—esque manner?)

———————

The beauty in "Ugliness" or "Commonplace" – e.g. a dusty road.

This, which has been recognized in prose, (I have exemplified it

often), has not been much done in verse. Crabbe had the

materials, but did not use them properly – i.e. make them   5

beautiful. – In painting the English Art Club attempts it.   (1905)

———————

<u>A calm day.</u> The air only moving enough to make a faint drone

through crevices of the window.

———————

Poem begins – Winter iced the ponds. May greened the trees –

<u>Lyrical Meth</u>   10

| Find a situ^n from exp^{ce} Turn to Ly^{cs} [From old notes. It

for a form of express^n that has been   appears to refer

used for a quite diff^t situ^n Use it   merely to form – an

(same sit^n from experience may be   easy way of finding

sung in sev^l forms.)   one]   15

———————

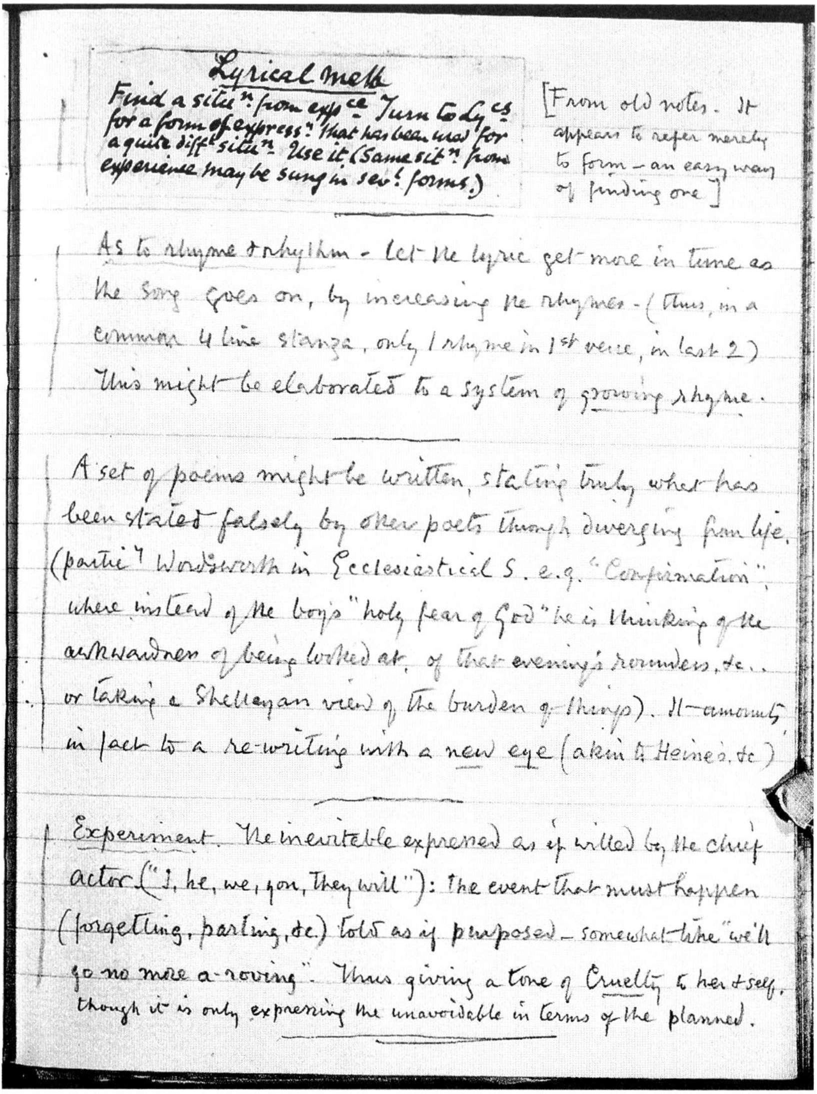

Lyrical meth

Find a situⁿ from expᶜᵉ Turn to Lyᶜˢ for a form of expressⁿ that has been used for a quite diffᵗ situⁿ. Use it (Same sitⁿ from experience may be sung in sevᶜ forms.)

[From old notes. It appears to refer merely to form — an easy way of finding one]

As to rhyme & rhythm — let the lyric get more in tune as the Song goes on, by increasing the rhymes — (Thus, in a common 4 line stanza, only 1 rhyme in 1st verse, in last 2) This might be elaborated to a system of growing rhyme.

A set of poems might be written, stating truly what has been stated falsely by other poets though diverging from life. (particⁿ Wordsworth in Ecclesiastical S. e.g. "Confirmation", where instead of the boy's "holy fear of God" he is thinking of the awkwardness of being looked at, of that evening's roundels, &c. . or taking a Shelleyan view of the burden of things). It amounts, in fact to a re-writing with a new eye (akin to Heine's, &c)

Experiment. The inevitable expressed as if willed by the chief actor ("I, he, we, you, They will"): the event that must happen (forgetting, parting, &c) told as if purposed — somewhat like "we'll go no more a-roving". Thus giving a tone of Cruelty to her & self, though it is only expressing the unavoidable in terms of the planned.

Figure 3.

As to rhyme & rhythm – let the lyric get more in tune as the song
goes on, by increasing the rhymes – (thus, in a common 4 line
stanza, only 1 rhyme in 1st verse, in last 2) This might be
elaborated to a system of growing rhyme.

———————

A set of poems might be written, stating truly what has been   5
stated falsely by other poets through diverging from life, (partic^y
Wordsworth in Ecclesiastical S. e.g. "Confirmation", where
instead of the boy's "holy fear of God" he is thinking of the
awkwardness of being looked at, of that evening's rounders, &c.
or taking a Shelleyan view of the burden of things). It amounts in   10
fact to a re-writing with a new eye (akin to Heine's, &c)

———————

Experiment. The inevitable expressed as if willed by the chief
actor – ("I, he, we, you, they will"): the event that must happen
(forgetting, parting, &c.) told as if purposed – somewhat like
"we'll go no more a-roving". Thus giving a tone of Cruelty to her   15
& self, though it is only expressing the unavoidable in terms of the
planned.

———————

"God" poems – continued from p . . . .

— "To the Lesser God." A new version of the Psalms. How to

satisfy that instinctive impulse to Praise, now that it cannot longer

be poured out to a supreme Being. – Qy: To the supreme slave,

5 the slave God, the subject God, the conditioned God, the Lesser

God, to God the Less, the Weaker: the tone is admiration,

glorification, to Him for his heroic hope & endeavour in His

fettered conditions. [a note made about 1906 from still earlier

notes]

10 — Another – Showing Him in a state of discomfort, or pain, the

changes of Nature being His efforts for relief.

— Cf. "The mischievous elevation of the quiet Will into volition

. . . and [discomfort] must again cease with the return of the Will

to its original state of self-enclosed peace." v. Hartm[n]. II.257.

15 — Series of Ghostly poems [like P–'s?]: a Fear of everything seen

(like Marky's). Combine "God", as "It", always haunting the poet,

who is ever on the qui vive for "It". Title, "It & I".   [about 1906]

"It's better to suppose ¶ That – wherefore no one knows – (he

did not consciously make the Tiger & the Lamb.)

The new moon, like a preened feather. Nov. 1909.

A new kind of poetry – that which depicts, leaving the
inference to the reader. (After looking at Goya's "Desastres").
[1905 or 6] [But would it be a new kind?]

———————

Why should I care [avoid Swin.s "A Leavetaking"]   5

Why should I care - - - - - - - - - -
                                                    [From old notes

   - - - - - - - - - - - - - - -
                                                    made about 190–.]
   - - - - - - - - - my pale concern

These women - - - - - - poor hearts burn

   - - - - - - - - adown this thoroughfare   10

                    Why should I care

———— // ————

Why shᵈ I {tell / sing} - - - - - - in [minor / broken] tones

            - - - - - - - racked their bones

                - - - - their sighs & tears

                - - their palpitating fears   15
   - - - - - - - - - - - - - {ell / ing}
            Why should I |tell / sing

———— // ————

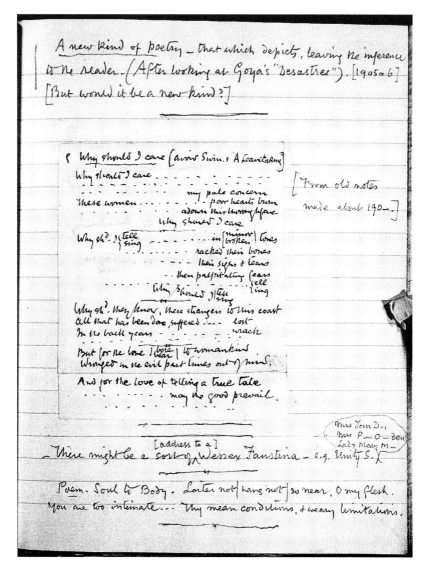

A new kind of poetry — that which depicts, leaving the inference
to the reader. (After looking at Goya's "Desastres"). [1905 or 6]
[But would it be a new kind?]

¶ Why should I care [avoir Swin.s 'A Leavetaking']
Why should I care . . . .
. . . . my pale concern   [From old notes
These women . . . . poor hearts burn   made about 190—.]
. . . . adown their history before
. . . . . . why should I care
Why sh⁰. I { tell . . . . in [minor / broken] tones
        { sing . . . . . . racked their bones
. . . . . . their sighs & tears
. . . then palpitating fears
. . . . why should I { tell
                    { sing
Why sh⁰. they know, these strangers to this coast
all that has been done, suffered . . . . lost
In the back years . . . . wrack
But for the love I { bore / bear } to womankind
Wronged in ne evil past times out of mind.
And for the love of telling a true tale
. . . . may the good prevail.

                                                    Mrs Tom D.,
                                            . Mrs P— O— den
            [address to a]   Lady Mary M—
There might be a sort of ∧ Wessex Faustina — e.g. Unity S.

Poem. Soul to Body. Loiter not / hang not / so near, O my flesh.
You are too intimate . . . thy mean conditions, & weary limitations.

Figure 4.

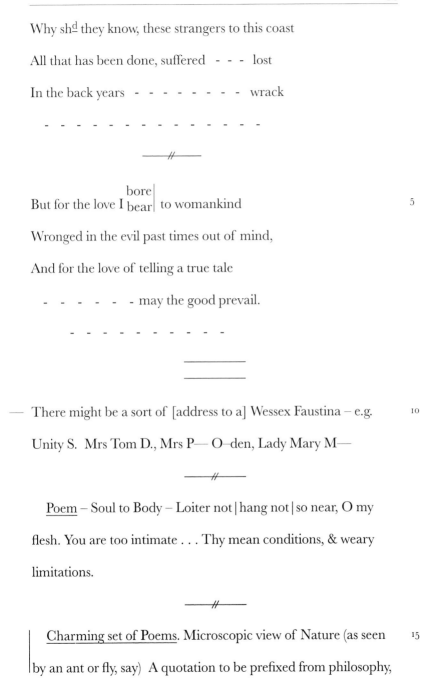

Why sh<u>d</u> they know, these strangers to this coast

All that has been done, suffered - - - lost

In the back years - - - - - - - - wrack

- - - - - - - - - - - - - -

————//————

But for the love I bore⎮bear⎮ to womankind   5

Wronged in the evil past times out of mind,

And for the love of telling a true tale

- - - - - - may the good prevail.

- - - - - - - - - -

————
————

— There might be a sort of [address to a] Wessex Faustina – e.g.   10

Unity S. Mrs Tom D., Mrs P— O–den, Lady Mary M—

————//————

<u>Poem</u> – Soul to Body – Loiter not⎮hang not⎮so near, O my

flesh. You are too intimate . . . Thy mean conditions, & weary

limitations.

————//————

<u>Charming set of Poems</u>. Microscopic view of Nature (as seen   15

by an ant or fly, say) A quotation to be prefixed from philosophy, or a brief statement in verse, to express that <u>size is entirely</u>

<u>relative</u> –

  Thus a leaf will be a <u>great green field or</u> down; frost-crystals

<u>swords & halberds</u>; mushrooms, tables; tombstones, façades.

5   (Could the title be "Once round the sun" ("& other verses" –)
or "The [Drama / Tale of the Year", "The [Scene / Spectacle of the year".) Also

lichen, chickweed, moss on bricks – (Mem. Lady in the

waterdrop.)   (about 1905)

_____

| Subjects known to the writer; unknown to the rest of the world.

_____

10 | Poems about <u>the other side of the story.</u> i.e. the other side of

things generally: before & after the usually chief incident, seems a

pregnant idea.   [about 1906]

_____

Simultaneousness – Mary Godwin coming out at dawn on July

—— 1814, to meet Shelley: J. Keats at H. at the moment: Byron at

15 —— doing what? W^worth at —— doing what? etc.   (1906)

_____

  People at Agricultural Show, or in a street – each bearing his

hope in his face; or their hopes hanging like lanterns in their
faces. Everybody had one of some kind.

———/———

The Ford. (Ballad).   ‖ [Meth Heads only]. – A pouring rain.
Young man takes up another (Anketell) one night, to drive him
through ford, the plank being washed away. In the middle he   5
pushes him in – he is drowned: the other sees his white face, &c.
Sister meets her brother, the driver of the gig, she having come
out with something over her head. B^r asks why she has come out
on such a night. She hesitatingly asks if he has met young
Anketell. He says significantly that he has, & wonders how she   10
can dare to ask for him: tells her he saw him go up by a ladder to
her chamber-window, &c. "And what if you did?" says she. He is
my dear husband: we were secretly married, not wishing my f^r to
know for the present. . . . (The ballad may end here, or go on:) B^r
goes back, looks for body in moonlight – corpse found next day.   15
She tells her f^r she is his wife – baby born. B^r says to baby when
alone "I have made thee fatherless". He never confesses: is a sad
man for life.
‖[Told in very jumpy rapid man^r of "Marie H . . ." Also may

combine with H–ne (Tod<u>er</u>). But have I not used the plot in "The Brother?" –]

———————

Crossing Ewelease from B. – (1906–8). Thinking how at B. we are always looking back at those who have gone before, who did

5 not look back in their time, but found the present all-sufficient. (Have I not already written something of this kind in verse?)

———————

Rejected from "The Dynasts.

•—— The Powers – Will, Doom, Time, or what not – accompany "The Poet" & explain scenes to him.

10 —— "The Eye of the Age" (good): also The Mage: The Soothsayer: The Spirit of Man: The Spirit of the Peoples: Spirit of Omniscience or Clairvoyance.

—— Spirits as Flies, Hares, &c.

—— Ghosts of dead nations or peoples. Assyria, Egypt, Greece,

15 Babylonia, Judaea &c. e.g. "Enter Egypt – "I cannot rest . . . something disturbs this Shade-land from above.' (Enter A., G., &c.) 'Ha – other sleepers wakened too thereby?'

—— Female figures, repres<u>g</u> Eng. France, Spain. &c, & America, (to whom the others explain.

— Slave Gods. – The Shaper, Travailer, or Genitress (Nature)

The Roller of the Years (Time?): The Portioner (Circumstance?)

The Silencer (Death): The Spirit of the Great Heart: The

Persister.   5

———//———

The Bitter in the Sweet. "Our sweet enemy" (France). (Cf.

"There's a'ways something"). e.g. "a beautiful sinister night" –

"brilliant mocking day" "joyous five months of {decaying fleeting green":

"artless hopefulness of the June trees that winter may come no

more": "my hated Love". &c –   10

———//———

"Subdramatic". . . . . ."dramatic thinking . . . combinations of life

or argument so vivid that it has dramatic force". Fotheringham's

"Studies in Browning."

———//———

| for in style of thought – not of expression.

Poem. "The man who had no friend" ☺ Auto. by John A–tell   15

sen. Cf. "The Two Leaders." Swin.

———//———

| The beautiful in the commonplace – "He [Swinburne] fails, as many poets failed – as Keats & Rossetti failed – to see the beautiful in everyday things. That power of seeking out new hidingplaces of romance – which Wordsworth & Browning had,

5   which Whitman had, which to-day is the possession of none save Mr Kipling [!] – that power Sw. had not. In the unsubstantial dreamworld of the poets he c^d find eternal beauty – he c^d not see that "Beauty is Truth, Truth Beauty, that is all."

Academy on Swinb^{ne} 17 April 1909.

———/———

10 | A man, in doubt about his religion, puts in one room images of Christ on the cross, Orpheus, Buddha, Confucius, Mahomet, &c. &c. In the night he hears them singing together. ☜ – "The virtuous Emp. Alex^r Severus set the image of Jesus in his lararium, together with that of Orpheus, Apollonius of Tyana".

15   &c. Times Lit. Sup. 24 June '09. (Rev^w of Glover's "Conflict of religions in Early Roman Empire" – 7/6.)

After the Monmouth rising, & the executions & distribution of bodies, a mistress of one who has been executed goes to the place where a quarter of him has been nailed up, takes down his arm brings it home & sleeps with it round her waist. [But has this some resemblance to Rizpah?]

———————

Imagine <u>everything</u> a person, with a character: e.g. "Fiddler June".

———————

<u>Ballad, or narrative poem</u>: Told in 1<u>st</u> person as "We" –   5

Two honourable men contrive to keep a married couple from eloping each with a lover. They succeed to their great satisfaction. "And we felt . . . & went to Church . . . And thanked God for what we had done, with a sense that we were somewhat better than other men are".   10

News that the husband has killed the wife in a quarrel. And when he was hanged we felt partly guilty of that woman's murder, & wondered why we had interfered.

———————

Poem. The Unborn & the Dead hold a meeting. The former have summoned the latter to ask their opinion on being born.   15

——/——

Poem. A man has written wicked or amorous verses, & has

been condemn$\underline{d}$ by the critics & public (e.g. Swin.). He repents, &
writes hymns before he dies. When he is dead people will not read
his hymns, but his profane poems.

". . . Speak of everyday things as the primitive barbarian would,
5 were he brought across them". Quoted in Q. Rev$\underline{w}$. [good for
poetry, if not for prose.]

Inverted accent – "Who seems to rule|realms by|her looks
alone". (Puttenham 1579). [C$\underline{d}$ every line be accented thus?]

Poem. "When I was myself" – ("When we were ourselves" &c) –
10 instancing each time when loving, kind, &c. "And I was myself
when," &c.

Poem – each verse ending "If I c$\underline{d}$ make them understand" –
last verse being that he "cannot make them understand." (metre.
Farewell; if ever fondest prayer.)

15   Sketch poems. "A painting can never be a complete
|representation of reality. . . . Line [a sketch] because limited

. . . has greater power" (condensed from Times Supp^t). An

illustration is supplied by Dorset children's rhyme: –

"Green grave O, green grave O, the grass is so green;

  The fairest young lady that ever was seen", &c.

———#———

The actors in the cruel tragedies of ancient ballads seem to feel   5

the emotions of the situation, but go on with the action as it were

automatically & by compulsion. ☙

———#———

Titles. "Poems of Occasion & . . . . ." | "Poems of Dreamery,

Doom, & . . ."   (about 1913)

———————

Poem. "I have been 7 yrs. in this grave. . . . The first year they   10

came 50 times. The second year . . . 20 times." &c [Mem H—e

124 Tod.]

———————

Having left something behind, a man feels his way into a

church at midnight. Is conscious of a congregation all round him;

or a marriage going on at the altar in costumes of 100, 200, 300,   15

years ago. &c

———————

— Dramatic poems. e.g. "What harm did she do to you?" in H—e

metre.

Another. (like "The Duel") The Death of Sir W. Hamilton. see

D. N. B. "Nelson".

———————

5   A woman Ariel. "Merrily, merrily shall I $\begin{cases} \text{lie} \\ \text{live} \end{cases}$ now under the

blossom" &c.

———/———

Cf Theocritus & the life at Bock^{n} when I was a boy – in the

wheatfield, at the well, cidermaking, wheat weeding, &c.

———/———

A letter comes in the handwriting & postmark of a lady long

10   since dead (e.g. the one I received like Graham Tomson's). He

fears to open it. (delayed in P. O. say)

———/———

Ancient Greek poem if required might be of people (children?)

making images of Diana: discuss Paul's preaching, or he is heard.

Or Scene in Ephesus, sculptors at work, etc. If child^{n}, one says,

15   "There's a man come", etc. The others, "What – no Diana? –

How foolish the man must be!" etc.

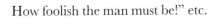

— Cerne Union – facing Giant. Pauper woman's Soliloquy.

———————

— Lady elopes with groom & marries him: arrive at home of his
parents. He is accidentally killed. She has child. Stays on in
cottage as one of the family. Is always going to leave: never does,   5
though she tries it once, & does not like what she sees, now foreign
to her habits: (Measure might be rhymed hexameters [mem:
Longf.'s Evangeline] Style St. & B.)   (old note.)

———————

"The sun had not shone for days & days" (begin a poem)

———————

"Mindsights" or other title, for set of poems in which the writer   10
continually sees an angel (or what not) in the way, as Balaam.

———————

Mystery Ballads – on some tragic situation; the ballad being
written round it, its actual nature being concealed all through.

———————

A day in a man's life treated as if it were 70 years & he an ephemerid – the events being very moving, & so ageing him.

––––––––––

Poem. "I thought before dawn . . . . | I thought at sunrise | I thought . . at noon . . . | I thought at night, when . . . . lights & cheer &c. | The hard unconquerable thing with me was to decide
5   which, &c.

––––––––––

  Content with injustice, in animals, birds, &c. Cf. Vaughan's "The Bird" – ("Many a sullen storm . . . . Rained on thy bed & harmless head.")

––––––//––––

  Poem by a Being who has lived hundreds of years, on how
10   belief in things contrary to the order of Nature has persisted, (in other words the Supernatural), as if there could be anything contrary to the order of Nature. Begin "When I lived in Egypt." To this Being the rise & fall of a dynasty is a few years of personal history.

––––––––––

15   Poem on the Incomprehensible. ☙ "The whole incomprehensible machine, from the holes between the stars to

the policy of the Allies"   Athenaeum.

————

<u>A timeless poem</u>. At the present date, for instance, Assyrian, Caesar, Christ, &c walk in at the door & talk. They may say there is no such thing as time; we mean to make it clear.

 Bear in mind in this connection Knight on the cliff (P. of Blue 5 Eyes) "Time shut up like a fan" &c [This might be motto of poem] Ozymandias, Legende des Siècles.

————

<u>Ballad</u> (in manner previously noted) of T. Cox & J<u>ma</u> Paul – mem. "Keith of R."

————//————

<u>Chorus of any future drama</u> – Ghosts of Helen, Potiphar's 10 wife, Bathsheba, Jael, Cleopatra, Faustina, M. Magdalene.

————/————

<u>Poems</u>. <u>Endings only</u>: beginning with And (Cf. "And like a dying lady" &c). These endings to be those of tragic lyrics, not written in full.

————/————

 A person sitting alone in a coach, a room, &c. The <u>faces</u> of 15 people look in, & bring tragic news scrap by scrap. Mode might be "K. of Rav$^{\underline{n}}$"

——/——

Xmas party at Lesnewth – Farm house: the clink of the locket. W$^{\underline{d}}$ this combine with "Burning the Holly?"

——//——

5 To see weather in process of making, & the way it is made. It may be seen completed anywhere, but to see it in making one must go to hills, cliffs, &c. She (Nature) first brings in the heavy atmosphere, then pulls a scroll of mist from over the hill, & stirs it in (like a housewife making a pudding) &c – [Last 2 lines]: –

10 "What mind, what force, what primary spring ¶ Has cared to do this useless thing?"

————

Rain has been much with me – A series of experiences of rain – e.g. by ewelease stile 12– p.m. – crossing F. Moor – in a crowd. &c

Woodyates Inn. or The Bagman's Story –

       17—

From|
  Of ⎱ first to last much have been seen
Aye!| first & last
           —— at Woodyates Inn

     - - outside - - & within   5

What chanced to me there

  Gets hold of me - - -

      ————

I rose - —— by   candlelight

  And hauled my pistols

  My money bags safe strapped   10

On second look - - my pistols

  —— seemed something strange

      ————

I looked at them again - -

  Their charges had been drawn

  At some time ere the dawn.   15

Reloading them ~~I reloaded them~~ without a word

  I ~~And~~ felt I must be gone   [why did I say nothing?

      ————   - - I was not a talkative

"Where is your husband. I said   man – burden of

                                 his story]

To the fair woman below

My landlady. "He had to go

Early this ~~Ea~~ morning." Very early, I said

And paid, & mounted, & left.

———

5 When I had ridden to

Just about the dawn
                              black crepe
A man with a blackened face

~~Came~~ Stood fronting me. "Your money or life!"
~~You are my~~
I drew & shot him dead

10   Woodyates

They took him back to the inn

And I followed ———

He was my landlord as I thought

And his wife wept.

———

15 And when I saw her comely face

Upturned despairingly

I thought, "O sad to see!

~~Cold~~ Could I elewise have saved my life

I'd not have widowed thee.

The Aged Bagman. | Near At Woodyates Inn.

I did it, yes I did it. It was near to Woodyates Inn

Blame me perhaps none can:

And yet – she was a handsome woman –   5
And ⌈ I was not a talkative man
     ⌊ he a pleasant man.

———

                                                    ⌈ frequented
The inn is where two counties meet, & once was │ patronized
   To   │ not unknown
   By the │ Queen, & George the King
           │ King & his family
And their daughters, in passing along the highway

   ⌈ To the town of their Sojourning   10
   ⌊ For their sojourn by the sea.

———

I was a thriving bagman in those years
                    one to ten
   With ⌈ gold & notes upon me
        ⌊ notes – one pound to ten
Often in high amount, for cheques to clear arrears
   Upon me, & gold   ⌈ - - - debtors
            common   ⌊   payments
   Were not so frequent then   15

[? Could it not continue in present tense.]

Meth: Sudden leaps of thought: eg:

"Marie H$\underline{\text{n}}$ is to the kirk gane

Wi' ribbons in her hair

The King thought mair of Marie H$^\text{n}$

5   Than ony that were there."

       ostler

This was known to the landlord, who having been a gentleman

of the road at an earlier day resolved to gain possession of it, for

the times were hard. But not wishing to commit the robbery at the

inn lest it should sow suspicion, he decided to do it on the road.

10 To make the deed a safe one he entered my room at night, &

                   | horsedung

drew the balls from my pistols, filling the barrels with | clay &

paper.

  When I rose in the morning & was about to stick my pistols in

my belt I fancied something was queer with them, & after a

15 minute found what it was. I reloaded them, saying nothing. Why

        ⌈ I was no —— ⌉ talking

did I say nothing? I know not. ⌊But I was never a⌋ talkative man.

  I mounted my horse, bade good bye cheerfully to my landlady,

who said her husband had gone a journey – he having in fact

     ~~I might have hinted to her that I was~~

gone ahead along my road. At the lonely corner by ——, where

———, he sprang out in front of me with his face blackened, saying

"your money or your life!" & holding up his pistol in my face. I

drew mine instantly, & shot him dead I might perhaps have cried

out to him that I had reloaded. But the moment was critical, & I

was never a talkative man."   5

/

She was a handsome woman

I c<u>d</u> have spared him for her sake

And when ⎰ white with grief & care
         ⎱   I saw her stand
I lost my heart to her forthwith

That she sh<u>d</u> have had her husband back   10

I would have given my hand.

The Leaf Fire. Making a fire of leaves in autumn – (indoors)

damp leaves. Sycamore, beech, &c – all since the spring.

The Present Tense – e.g. in ballads, &c.

"It dispenses with all question & answer – all explanation – what   15

we are witnessing is not the drama down below, but is the drama

up here in the soul of this strange marvellous prophet (Carlyle)."

———————

Paean to the $\begin{bmatrix} \text{Conditioned} \\ \text{Lesser God} - \\ \text{Thwarted} \end{bmatrix}$

A Psalm of Praise, the tone being one of admiration,

glorification of Him for his heroic hopes, attempts to save, &

other endeavours, under His fettered conditions. [copied from an

5 old note of many years ago.]

––––––––

ℙ "My heart beats out of tune" ☙ (on anxious love &c)

––––––––

? "Two Trees" – Twelve years & over	At first with bare knees
I walked by Two Trees	- - - - - & after
That stood side by side	My sweetheart might please
On the slope of the leaze	- - - - - - - -

- - - - - - - -

Good tragic ballad. A woman who has been seduced finds that

the man has married. She kills him. Finds then that his wife is her

sister (whom he has also seduced?)   1869. June 15.

––––––––

15 A suffering God: an afflicted God: a self-mortifying God: a self-

chastizing, self-chastening God: a self-punishing God (i.e. causing defects & pains in a world which is a manifestation of himself.) –

1901. Feb.

———//———

? <u>Moods towards Nature.</u>

      In times of - - - - -   I censured her

                             I censured her   5

      - - - - - - - - - -

      And then I grew to reverence her

                       To reverence her
                                     ⎰weaves
[Nothing disturbs her equanimity – she secretly ⎱spins on]

      - - - - - - - - - - -   10

      But now I have grown to pity her

                       Pity her . . .

[I think of her pathetic patience, her mismated beings, her
misplanted seeds, her destroyed fruit. Still she plods on. Her
illogical want of foresight in so creating that she cannot save both   15
the lion & | his prey | be merciful to his prey. Till she seems a
pale-faced seampstress, shop-confined, who never weeps nor
smiles.

———/———

<u>The Lady who declined</u>. [Style S. & B.]

<u>Prefatory note</u>. It happened once that a lady was so fascinated by the strains of a violin played by her groom in the harness room that she eloped with & married him. Her father cast her off & she

5   sang about the streets to her husband's fiddle for a living. Otherwise: –

Miss Rosa Delalynde dau. of Sir Hugh D. elopes with & marries her groom – having first been attracted to him by the sweet strains of his violin as he practised in the harness room.

10   In a week or two they have to consider how to live: a letter from her father: he throws her off & will not help them.

They go to the husb$^{d's}$ parents' cottage, that she may stay there while he looks about for occupation.

He goes away to search. Is accidentally killed   She stays on at

15   cottage. At first strange, but she gets accustomed to cottage ways, though she thought she could not. Decides to leave somehow. Then thinks she will stay till her baby is born.

She grows to like her f. & m. in law (he may be carpenter or mason)   She joins in household work, but is always intending to

20   appeal again to her f.

Thinks she will wait till the baby is bigger, & has to be put to

school. He gets bigger. She thinks he may as well go to the village

school, for the rudiments Postpones going to her f.ᵗ – Appeals to

the boy to go. He says he w.ᵈ rather stay & learn his grandf.ᵗ'ˢ

trade. Her f. dies. Boy learns trade. She gets old as a cottage   5

woman. Her son is carpenter on her f's estate, wh. passed to a

cousin.

⌈Cousin may invite her. She unhappy there everything seeming⌉

⌊strange. Goes back to cottage where she feels quite at home ⌋

   <u>Begin</u>:   O the strains of that violin   10

            From the harness-room, where, close shut in

            He practised, & her ear did win.

                  ———

            She was the daughter of the house

            And he the groom: ~~of~~ her heart's carouse
                all
            She kept ~~it~~ silent as a mouse.   15

               &c

? [1863–7]   161

July 18. <u>Poem</u> (ballad metre) [good]

     rough outline –

     1. "I sat me down in a foreign town,

         And looked across the way:

                  was   ⌈ sitting
         At a window there ~~sat~~ a lady |-fair
                        ⌊ leaning

         Far] fairer than the day.

         [Rhyme only 2nd & 4th lines]

     2. "Twelve ~~days~~ blessed days she won my gaze

         Twelve days she looked at me", &c

—————#—————

— He meets her at P. O. & finds her with letter to him – finds she

is the anonymous correspondent he has loved so long – when she

is out he follows, she eludes him – asks the landlord of the hotel

who she is – says she & her sister are staying there – but he has

                                            his
only spoken with sister – not with the beautiful one – He tells

~~my~~ tale that she is the woman he has been looking for so long. He

tells her name – finds she belongs to an ancient English family.

                                  lover
On a little pressing he allows ~~me~~ to see her room – it is here he

finds a letter directed to him, & pps. the discovery that she is the

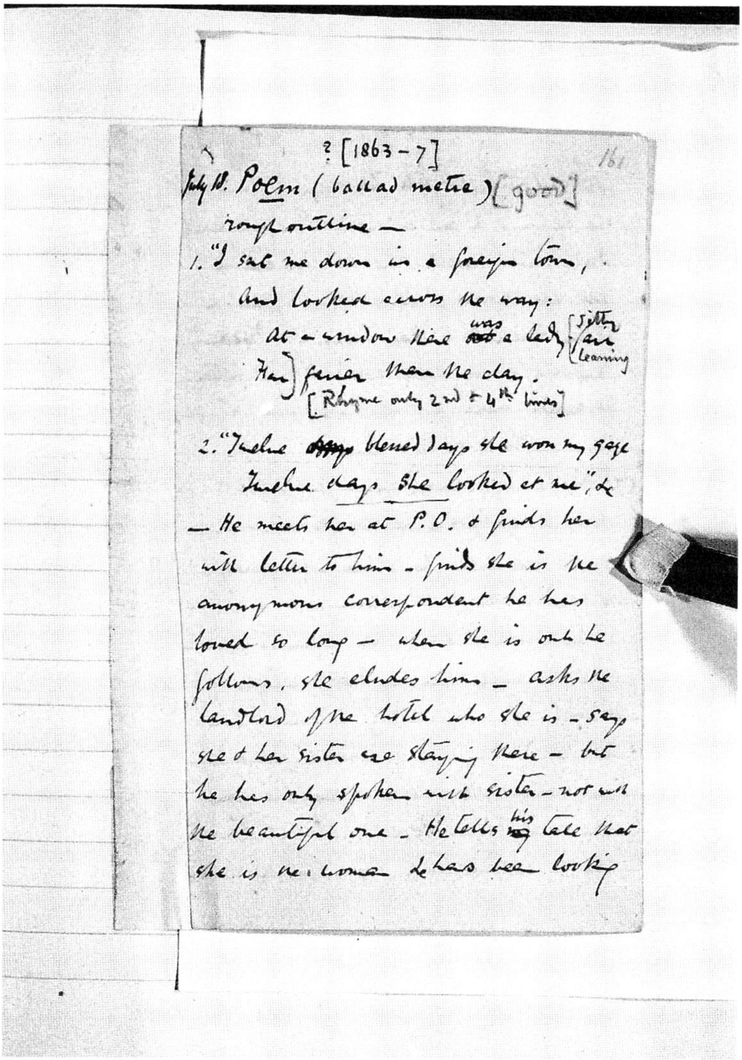

? [1863 – 7]

July 11. Poem (ballad metre) [good]

rough outline —

1. "I sat me down in a foreign town,
And looked across the way:
at a window there *was* a lady [sitting / and leaning]
Her/fairer than the day.
[Rhyme only 2nd & 4th lines]

2. "Twelve ~~days~~ blessed days she won my gaze
Twelve days she looked at me" &c
— He meets her at P.O. & finds her
with letter to him – finds she is the
anonymous correspondent he has
loved so long — when she is out he
follows, she eludes him — asks the
landlord of the hotel who she is – says
she & her sister are staying there — but
he has only spoken with sister – not with
the beautiful one – He tells *his* tale that
she is the woman he has been looking

Figure 5.

correspondent had better be made here – & the story told to the

landlord, as they stand.

    She always eludes him – face sad – & too thoughtful – he sees

her weeping, &c – her sister begs him to go away. He sends

5 proposal of marriage.

    She writes & says her sister is opposed but she will marry him

secretly – if he trusts her sufficiently to meet her at the door of

——'s church, at such an hour. He agrees, & goes. She comes –

she is trembling – He clasps her & kisses her for the first time.

10 This is in the door.

163

He

They see the priest waiting (through an open door) I aske asks

her to speak to him – she takes out her tablets, ivory, as she stands

his   him

with ~~my~~ arm round her – & writes – that she has loved ~~me~~ too

15 well – could not help coming – in hope – That a curse is upon

her – she is <u>dumb</u>.

    He jumps from her in horror –. she falls – He goes away –

thinks of her – returns – dead.

    (or the meeting might be merely a first lover's meeting, which

his

20 she grants on ~~my~~ urging it by a note)

/   named a

"Six times I ~~begged to nam~~ trysting place,

    Six times replièd she:
                love   likewise
"Perhaps I prize thy ~~form six times replied~~

    But to meet – it cannot be!"

[This ballad was never finished]   5

Shades of the Lyrists

<u>Scene</u>. <u>Night. A lamp-lit room</u>. <u>Moonlight out of doors</u>.

<u>Tune played within</u> [<u>by blind player</u>?] "When he who adores thee".

<u>Dead face of Moore rises</u> outside window pane or voice of Moore

afar. [Bromham: village n^r Devizes]   10

<u>Moore</u>.   Why do you call me thus

        I have said my say

      Glad, loving, mournful, tragic, frivolous,

        And I'd away!

<u>Blind player</u>.   I feel a cold damp draught with an earthy smell.   15

        Whence does it come? Listeners, I pray you tell?

<u>Listeners</u>.   Change the tune! (<u>Player stops</u>. <u>Face disappears</u>)

(Or: the <u>scene</u> may be thus: Traveller who has lost his way looks

through keyhole: people all round room (handsome young
witches?); blind player: dumb listener: candles: red wine: & as
above.)

––––––––––

<u>Tune played within</u>. "When we two parted."

5 <u>Dead face of Byron rises</u> outside window-pane; or voice of B.
afar.

<u>Byron</u>.   Why do you so disquiet me [In Hucknall Ch. yd. lying]

I have said my say

A hundred years ago such moods could be

10   Mine night & day

But this breast throbs no more

As of yore!

Player stops. Face disappears

<u>Tune played within</u>. "O Brignall Banks". [Dryburgh Abbey

15 aisle]

<u>Dead face of Scott rises outside window-pane, or voice of Scott
afar. on N. wind</u>

<u>Scott</u>.   Why do you call me up | forth | ?

&c.

Or: instead of phantoms being visible to reader & listeners, they

are only visible to a child who is present (who has been given

snag $\left\{\begin{array}{l}\text{gin.}\\\text{wine?}\end{array}\right.$). Child describes each phantom – they say: "It's   5

Byron! "Listen." (<u>Voice of Byron</u>)

––––––––––

<u>Other characters raised</u> 1 Swinburne. 2 Browning. 3 Tenny$^{\underline{n}}$

4. Moore: 5 Wordsworth: 6 Scott: 7 Byron: 8. Shelley (rather

faint) 9. Keats: 10 Milton (faint): 11 Shakespeare (very faint)

<u>Or, suppose musicians entirely</u>: –   10

Blue Danube = (Strauss): Gondoliers = (Sullivan) Mocking

Bird (Christy) Trovatore (Verdi): William Tell (Rossini):

Tannhauser (Wagner): &c

Annotations

References to the text of 'Poetical Matter' are by page and line numbers.

3.1–2 *This book . . . T.H.*: inscribed in ink over erased pencil, possibly in the red ink reported by Purdy as having been used for these same words on the paper jacket.

3.4–5 *I . . . experimented on)*: written over largely irrecoverable erasures. At 3.4 the concluding erased word is 'unwritten', evidently used in the same sense as 'not been experimented on'.

3.7 *Ap.̣ 3. 1873*: this date presumably relates to the point in TH's sequence of pocket-books (see Introduction) at which he began transferring selected entries into 'Poetical Matter'. That the earliest dated of the immediately following unerased notes is from 1876 is evidently a consequence of some re-ordering of the 'Poetical Matter' entries after its inception; see next annotation. After TH had stopped working more or less chronologically through his pocket-books, he continued to refer to them on a less systematic basis, often invoking only 'old note' but sometimes returning more specifically to notes dated even earlier than those in the initial sequence; see 33.17, 34.5, 34.14 (the earliest dated note, headed 'Aug 26. 1868'), 72.14, and 76.1 (the earliest dated entry, headed '? [1863–7]').

3.8–18 *Titles . . . Speaks in Verse*: written over three erased notes, of which the first (3.8–12) is essentially irrecoverable, the second (3.15) reads 'Dance of Hailstones in storm' and was reinscribed at 13.1 in a space itself created by an erasure, and the third (located just below 3.18) begins 'Dance of hailstones on bridge', continues with several irrecoverable words in the same line, and concludes with a bracket enclosing a list of eight irrecoverable but evidently alternative single-word readings; see frontispiece. Prior to being transferred to the opening page of 'Poetical Matter', the complete list of titles had been entered (and subsequently erased) at 13.10 in another space created by an erasure. At one point TH began to list the titles on the page (otherwise unused) that faces the opening page; the now erased text reads:

> Suggested Titles –
> The Look of Life | Lives
> Poems <probably> final

It is not clear when TH began his list of titles, but the majority of them appear to be of late date. 'Poems Imaginative & Incidental: with Songs and Trifles' was TH's 29 July 1925 suggestion, 'for want of a better title', for the collection published in November of that year as *Human Shows, Far Phantasies, Songs, and Trifles* (*CL* vi. 341; see also *CL* vi. 347–8), and the presence here of 'Poems imaginative & incidental' is reflective of its not having been so used, hence remaining available for possible future use. 'Poems probably final' clearly envisages what did in fact become TH's last poetry collection, and, as the draft title-page for *Winter Words in Various Moods and Metres* (Peter Old) so interestingly shows, he arrived at that title only after considering several variations on titles listed here: e.g., 'Last Poems', 'Winter Flowers',

'Wintry Things Thought in Verse with Other Poems', 'A Wintry Voice in Various Moods & Metres', 'A Wintry Voice Speaks in Verse', and 'Winter Words in Various Moods & Metres' (cf. *CPW* iii. 322–3).

OED Online defines 'mind-sight' as the 'ability of the mind to understand, imagine, or penetrate; (also) a mental picture'. Here (at 3.10) and in, e.g., 'The Mother Mourns' (*CPW* i. 145), TH seems to be using 'mindsight' in the first sense, but later in 'Poetical Matter' (63.10) and in, e.g., 'To a Motherless Child' (*CPW* i. 86), the emphasis is on things seen only in the mind.

3.19 *Toll gate*: TH here invokes the old Fordington Moor toll-gate, on the main road just east of Dorchester, as the setting for a series of imaginary and somewhat macabre situations that might be treated in a poem or poems. The bracketed references are to Keats's 'La Belle Dame sans Merci' (cf. 10.4) and to the Scottish ballad 'The Wife of Usher's Well' (cf. 14.7–8 and 28.4). For Fordington Moor, see 66.12 n.; for the toll-gate itself, see *Facts*, 59–60, and Jo Draper, *Dorchester Past* (Chichester: Phillimore, 2001), 28. 'Or separated . . . night.' is a late addition.

4.2 *Needles light*: the light shining from the Needles lighthouse at the western extremity of the Isle of Wight would have been visible from the Dorset coast at Swanage, where TH and ELH lived from July 1875 to March 1876 (*LW* 110–11 and *BR* 164–5).

4.4 *Old incapable people*: another note probably made in Swanage, by this date already well known as a coastal resort.

4.7 *[Erasure]*: the original three-line note is essentially irrecoverable.

4.8 *Late autumn*: 'Em.' is ELH; the garden is presumably the one attached to the house in Sturminster Newton (see 5.8 n.) to which she and TH had moved by the autumn of 1876. TH subsequently adapted her remark for inclusion in *The Woodlanders*, ch. 30 (*W* 260–1).

4.11 *Dead man*: the source and perhaps the subject of the anecdote would seem to have been Elizabeth Vincent of Puddletown (aged 17 in the 1851 census), daughter of George Vincent. TH's first cousin Christopher Hand married a Jane Vincent in 1862.

4.13 *[Erasure: largely recovered]*: the recoverable text reads:

> Melbury man – very tall: made his coffin fearing the carpenter would not make it long enough. Kept it under his bed. His brother, also tall, died first: he had it: the Melbury man made another for himself. (Hear a man tapping every night in house opposite < > – [at work making it.] [Another brother, or son, dies & has coffin: man has to make another for himself: drowned at sea?]

TH drew a line around the final square-bracketed sentence. This note (cf. the length-of-coffin anecdote at *LW* 164) was developed into 'The Three Tall Men' (*CPW* iii. 187–8), first collected in *Winter Words* following prior publication in the *Daily Telegraph* (Purdy, 261). That the poem was one of TH's last compositions is indicated by the survival (in addition to the *Winter Words* manuscript at Queen's College, Oxford) of two draft manuscripts containing variant readings, one (DCM) with the first of its two leaves written on the verso of a printed form that included the date 28 September 1926, and the other (Colby College) entitled 'The Two Tall Men' and written on the verso of a promotional circular dated 24 August 1927 (see

CPW iii. 324–5). For other *Winter Words* poems clearly originating in erased or struck-through 'Poetical Matter' notes, see 6.8 n., 26.11–13 n., and 37.2 n.

5.1   *Eyes of Mediterranean blue*: evidently said by rather than about ELH, whose eyes TH described as 'deep grey' (*LW* 77; cf. 'After a Journey', *CPW* ii. 60). The image seems to have struck TH as original, and ELH may have encountered an early occurrence of 'Mediterranean blue' as a colour description, especially for cloth, that became common only later in the century.

5.2   *Calm day*: this note is repeated almost word for word at 47.7–8, though without the added reference to Swanage itself.

5.4   *[Excision]*: to the right of the shorthand symbol almost half of the leaf has been cut away at the bottom, presumably indicating that the excised material had included a note developed into a poem—conceivably a note similar to or identical with the surviving note at *LW* 111, an evident source for 'Once at Swanage' (*CPW* iii. 103), first published in *Human Shows*.

5.5   *Rushy Pond*: Rushy Pond itself is on the heath not far from the Higher Bockhampton cottage, where TH had evidently been visiting his parents. His lying among the camomiles and shepherd's thyme clearly refers back to his own youthful memories and to his sympathy with the quietist habits of his father: see *LW* 20, 26, and *BR* 26. The poem 'Childhood among the Ferns' (*CPW* iii. 199–200), first collected in *Winter Words* following prior publication in the *Daily Telegraph* (Purdy, 261), was perhaps prompted by this note, and cf. the reference to 'shepherds' thyme' in 'The Ballad of Love's Skeleton' (*CPW* iii. 269), also in *Winter Words*.

5.8   *At S. Newton*: the Hardys arrived in Sturminster Newton in north Dorset on 3 July 1876 and rented a newly built semi-detached house named Riverside Villa: see *LW* 114–15 and *BR* 171–2. The note itself is also included in the 'Memoranda I' notebook (*PN* 19).

5.12   *At Blandford*: Blandford Forum is a handsome market-town situated on the River Stour some 9 miles to the south-east of Sturminster.

6.5   *[Erasure: largely recovered]*: the recoverable text (apparently not developed into a poem) reads:

> The <beams of the living> room of cottage: & the nails for hats, with <minuscule> stains from their wet brims.   (1877)

6.8   *[Erasure: largely recovered]*: the recoverable text reads:

> Very wet windy day: rooks & pigeons penetrated by the rain: dishevelled vultures – gaunt, shabby, & <   >.   (1877)

This erased note, along with those at 6.11 and 7.1, was closely drawn upon in TH's composition of 'An Unkindly May' (*CPW* iii. 174), subtitled '(1877)' in manuscript and first collected in *Winter Words* following prior publication in the *Daily Telegraph* (Purdy, 261). The poem was one of TH's last, evidently completed on 27 November 1927, only a fortnight before he found himself unable to work in his study and took to his bed for his final illness; see at *LW* 478 FEH's entry for 27 November 1927, itself a shortened version of her diary entry for that date (DCM, *CPW* iii. 323), and *BR* 529. These erased notes for 'An Unkindly May' (see also 6.11 n., 7.1 n., 27.4 n., and 51.2 n.) provide a unique glimpse into TH's creative processes, especially his late use of 'Poetical Matter' material; see Introduction. For other *Winter Words* poems clearly originating in erased or struck-through 'Poetical Matter' notes, see 4.13 n., 26.11–13 n., and 37.2 n.

6.11   *[Erasure: largely recovered]*: the recoverable text reads:

> Nature's mood is not always commendable. This is a sour spring day: dirty clouds carried lumberingly along by a <scraping sour wind:> trees <creak like> rusty cranes: buds have tried to open but have pinched themselves together again: birds inharmonious & <   >: sun frowns, a <dark   > light.   (1877)

Another source for the language and imagery of 'An Unkindly May'; see preceding annotation.

6.12–14   *Sunday. . . . (1877)*: an apparent indication that TH was a regular church-goer at this date.

6.15   *Man comes to terrace*: a more detailed version of this note, dated 1 May 1877, appears at *LW* 117. Riverside Villa is the more northerly of a pair of semi-detached houses that stand on a bluff (TH's 'terrace') with a view westwards over the River Stour and the meadows beyond. Cf. TH's 'Overlooking the River Stour', first published in *Moments of Vision* in 1917 (*CPW* ii. 223 and Purdy, 199).

7.1   *Faces . . . length of*: written over an erased note beginning '— Windy cold evening in May'. Another note drawn upon for 'An Unkindly May'; see 6.8 n.

7.3   *Reeds by the River Stour*: for a more extended note on the Stour at Sturminster Newton, dated July 1876, see *LW* 115.

7.5   *At Bagber*: TH knew and admired the Revd William Barnes (1801–86), the Dorset dialect poet (see 45.10 n.), and his visit to Barnes's birthplace alongside the old droveway across Bagber Common, just west of Sturminster Newton, was clearly a gesture of respect. The house in which Barnes was born seems to have been pulled down around the middle of the nineteenth century, and nothing even of what TH saw can now be recognized at the site, itself locatable only by map references.

7.9   *On board the Gravesend boat*: Gravesend, on the south bank of the River Thames some 20 miles east of London, served as the city's 'boundary port', where incoming ships picked up pilots and went through customs procedures. It was also a popular pleasure resort, known for its gardens, taverns, and locally caught shrimp, and much visited by day-trippers using the regular steamer service to and from London. TH's note appears to have been based upon an excursion of this nature, presumably in the company of ELH, shortly after their move to Tooting, in south London, in March 1878 (*LW* 123).

7.15   *At K.*: numerous Dorset villages and hamlets bear names beginning with 'K', but the intimacy of the information would seem to indicate a source fairly close to Higher Bockhampton, where TH's parents continued to live—perhaps the group of cottages known as Higher Kingston and located just beyond Higher Kingston farm.

8.1   *At Tooting*: the address to which the Hardys moved on 22 March 1878 was 1 Arundel Terrace, Trinity Road, Tooting, the end-house of a three-storey Victorian terrace. The note is evidently related to the poem 'Beyond the Last Lamp' (*CPW* ii. 20–1), first published in 1911 and subsequently collected in *Satires of Circumstance* (1914), but since TH at this point in the compilation of the notebook was fascinated by reflections and other light effects (see next two notes and cf. 4.2–3, 5.12–16, 14.10, 14.11–17, 26.4–6, *PN* 11, *LW* 141), he was perhaps seizing on the note's conclusion, 'drops of rain cause flashes', not invoked in 'Beyond the Last Lamp'.

8.3 *Going downstairs*: although this note and the next are again concerned with effects of light, they also provide glimpses of the interior of 1 Arundel Terrace.

8.5 *Shines*: affectionate though this note's depiction of ELH appears to be, it has to be read in the context of the poem 'A January Night (1879)' (*CPW* ii. 204–5), first published in *Moments of Vision* (1917), and of TH's unusually explicit comment that it was an incident at Tooting early in 1879 that caused the couple 'to begin to feel that "there had past away a glory from the earth"' (*LW* 128; TH's quotation is from Wordsworth's 'Ode: Intimations of Immortality').

8.15 *Horse standing by river*: perhaps Bob, TH's father's horse, used to transport building supplies and mentioned in TH's account of his two-week visit to his parents at Bockhampton in February 1879 (*LW* 128–30).

9.3 *returning from the Derby*: the 1879 Derby was run at the Epsom racecourse on 28 May, *The Times* of 29 May noting that the weather had been 'most unfortunate' (p. 10). Epsom was accessible from Tooting, and TH went again to the Derby in May 1880 (*LW* 141–2).

9.5 *Sunset*: this note, almost identically phrased and dated 2 March 1879, is also included in the 'Memoranda I' notebook (*PN* 20); cf. 9.7 n.

9.6 *Bock*[n]: this note and the next were evidently made during the visit to Bockhampton and Weymouth paid by TH and (for part of the time) ELH in late August 1879 (*LW* 132–3 and *BR* 192–3).

9.7 *Wet at Weymouth*: this note is closely replicated in the 'Memoranda I' notebook (*PN* 20); cf. 9.5 n.

9.9 *Sir J. Reynolds' portraits*: TH would have seen numerous portraits by Sir Joshua Reynolds (1723–92; *OxfordDNB*) in the art section of the 1862 International Exhibition and in some of the Old Masters exhibitions mounted in London each winter by the Royal Academy. A brief mention of Reynolds occurs in TH's early 'Schools of Painting' notebook (*PN* 113), and 'the numerous faded portraits by Sir Joshua Reynolds' are referred to in his short story 'Fellow-Townsmen' (*Wessex Tales*, 137). For the causes of deterioration in Reynolds's paintings, see Ian McIntyre, *Joshua Reynolds: The Life and Times of the First President of the Royal Academy* (London: Allen Lane, 2003), 124–6, 233, and 276.

9.11 *[Erasure]*: the original two-line note is essentially irrecoverable.

9.12–14 *L*[d] *Brougham . . . M*[c]*Carthy*: TH knew Justin McCarthy (1830–1912; *OxfordDNB*), the Irish politician and historian, and is here summarizing from McCarthy's *A History of Our Own Times from the Accession of Queen Victoria to the General Election of 1880*, 4 vols. (London: Chatto & Windus, 1879–80), iv. 254, a sentence about two former Lord Chancellors, Henry Peter Brougham, 1st Baron Brougham and Vaux (1778–1868; *OxfordDNB*), and John Singleton Copley, Baron Lyndhurst (1772–1863; *OxfordDNB*): 'It is said that in his failing, later years [Brougham] often directed his coachman to drive him to Lord Lyndhurst's house, as if his old friend and gossip were still among the living.'

9.15   *At the end of a historical play*: a powerfully imagined idea derived from the intimate knowledge of Shakespeare's works that TH demonstrated in his early 'Studies, Specimens' notebook, in the markings and annotations made in all ten volumes of *The Dramatic Works of William Shakespeare*, ed. Samuel Weller Singer (London: Bell & Daldy, 1856), now in the DCM, and in numerous allusions throughout his own writings.

10.4   *"Belle Dame"*: another reference to Keats's 'La Belle Dame sans Merci' (cf. 3.20).

10.5   *The gale of last week*: evidently the gale of 30 April, with winds 'almost reaching the force of a hurricane in the Channel', reported in *The Times*, 1 May 1882, 6. The Hardys had moved from Tooting in June 1881 to the east Dorset town of Wimborne Minster. That their new garden was full of 'all sorts of old-fashioned flowers' (*LW* 154) has perhaps some bearing on TH's next note.

10.8   *Old house at Fordingbridge*: Fordingbridge is a small Hampshire town some 15 miles north-east of Wimborne, but it is not clear whether TH actually stayed there from 12 to 15 May 1882 or simply paused on his way to or from somewhere further afield. A note dated 13 May 1882 speaks approvingly of 'The slow meditative lives of people who live in habitual solitude' (*LW* 158). 'Miss Jones' has not been found, but was perhaps Miss Johns of Rowlands, Wimborne; Mr Chislett was Henry O. Chislett, land agent, of West Borough, Wimborne.

10.17   *Saw their backs*: the backs TH saw were those of Henry Hardy, his brother, and Jemima Hardy, their mother, and although the note falls within a sequence of entries for 1882, it seems likely to have dated, as indicated by the retrospectively added '1883 – ', from after TH and ELH had moved to Dorchester in June 1883 (*LW* 167).

11.2–3   *A blackbird has eaten*: an almost identically phrased note, dated August 1882, occurs at *LW* 158–9.

11.5   *A Satire of Circumstance*: the narrative here appears to be of TH's own invention, but it is not clear whether the term 'Satire of Circumstance' (as in the title of *Satires of Circumstance*, published in 1914) was part of the original entry or introduced only when the note was being copied.

11.10   *Another*: a 'satire of circumstance' drawing upon the life of Robert Eyers of Blandford Forum, whom TH seems to have known and admired. Eyers, earlier a postilion (see *PN* 23), became landlord of the Crown Inn in Blandford and operator of horse-drawn coach services to Wimborne, Dorchester, and elsewhere until finally driven out of business by the coming of the railway to Blandford itself in the early 1860s.

11.16   *At Dorchester*: the girls' elementary school in Bell Street (now part of Icen Way), at which TH's sister Mary Hardy taught, was within a short distance both of the original location of the Dorset County Museum and of the building next to St Peter's Church to which the Museum moved in 1884.

12.8   *Courting*: TH believed that his maternal great-grandparents John Swetman and Maria Childs had lived in houses close to each other on the outskirts of the north Dorset village of Melbury Osmond and courted, as he says, from bedroom window to bedroom window, although in his sketch (DCM) of Townsend, the still-standing Swetman house, the intervening distance seems too great for conversations of any intimacy to have been carried on. That there was family opposition to the romance can be inferred from the couple's having subsequently married, apparently without parental approval, in the distant Dorset seaport of Poole. For references to the Swetman and Childs families, see *LW* 10–12 and *BR* 14–15, 258.

12.10 *The 3 sounds*: domestic industries were common in Dorset villages until well into the nineteenth century, and many of the women of Melbury Osmond (the 'M.' of this note) were employed as spinners, especially of a strong linen called tick, used particularly for mattress covers, and a coarse linen called dowlas. TH's manuscript compilation, 'Country Songs of 1820 onwards | Killed by the Comic Song of the Music Hall' (DCM) includes 'Fragment of a quaint Ballad | Sung by Wessex weavers about 1820'. See Hutchins, iv. 439, and J. C. Townsend, *Melbury Osmond— Its Church & People* (Melbury Osmond, 1960), 9–10.

12.13 *Still life scene*: Thomas Lock worked Higher Kingston farm (part of the Kingston Maurward estate), just to the north-east of Dorchester. Although the spring-fed pond—quite large, to judge from surviving photographs—has now disappeared, its location, at the point where the lane to the farm met the main London road, is still identifiable.

13.1 *Dance . . . storm.*: originally located at 3.15 (see n.) and here inscribed over an irrecoverable one-line erasure.

13.2 *[Excision]*: approximately one-sixth of the leaf cut away at the bottom.

13.3 *The Doctor*: evidently a story in oral circulation that probably reached TH through his sister Mary, who had taught in the village school at Piddlehinton (north-west of Puddletown) during the early 1870s and kept in touch with people she had known there. Reed-drawing (or reed-pulling) was a village industry in several parts of Dorset: 'The straw was placed between wooden presses and each stalk was withdrawn by hand, the ears being cut off and the straw made into bundles. This was done at piece-work rate in the evening' (quoted in Marianne R. Dacombe (ed.), *Dorset Up Along and Down Along* (Dorchester: Dorset Federation of Women's Institutes, 1935), 53). Cf. *Tess of the d'Urbervilles*, ch. 43 (*W* 369–73).

13.10 *[Erasure: largely recovered]*: it was in the second through seventh lines of this seven-line space, itself created by an earlier (now irrecoverable) erasure, that TH inscribed and then erased the prospective poetry volume titles now located on the notebook's first page (see 3.8–18 n.).

13.11 *Two Trees*: evidently the name—perhaps specific to TH—of a local landmark; it reappears as the title of the draft poem present at 72.7–11. 'Drong' is defined in William Barnes's glossary of the Dorset dialect as 'A narrow way between two hedges or walls'.

14.1 *Lambing House*: probably to be identified with 'Eweleaze Barn', south-west of Higher Kingston farm, as located and named on 6-inch Ordnance Survey maps of 1963. An 'eft' is a newt or (as here) a small lizard.

14.6 *Mrs Ashley*: the Hon. Anthony Henry Ashley, third son of the 6th Earl of Shaftesbury, had represented Dorchester as a Member of Parliament and served as Deputy Lieutenant of the county, but when he died, aged 51, in 1858, he was buried in London, at Kensal Green. Many years later (apparently in late 1884 or early 1885) his widow, the Hon. Jane Frances Ashley of Stratton Manor, just north-west of Dorchester, had his body exhumed and re-interred in the churchyard at

Stratton. She subsequently took much interest in Stratton church itself, funding a
radical reconstruction of which TH deeply disapproved (*CL* i. 220–1, vii. 115–16),
and was buried there alongside her husband at her death in 1893. For 'The Wife of
Usher's Well', cf. 3.20 and 28.4. '[the grave – my cottage, my cellar –]' is a late addi-
tion, presumably directed toward the generation of a possible poem.

14.10   *Sparks from skid*: stones in or on the roads could readily strike sparks from
the iron rims fitted to the wooden wheels of contemporary farm waggons.

14.11   *A camp at night*: TH's positive response to this encounter on Stinsford Hill
was perhaps related to the strong interest in gypsies and their culture demonstrated
by such friends of his as the American writer Charles Leland (see *LW* 132). 'July' is
a late addition.

14.18   *A wedding*: the Dorchester wedding on 20 August 1885 of Emily Frances
Ashley, daughter of the Hon. Jane Frances Ashley of Stratton Manor and of the
late the Hon. Anthony Henry Ashley (see 14.6 n.), to the widower Henri de Satge,
third son of the Vicomte de Satge. John Floyer (1811–87), of Stafford House, Con-
servative Member of Parliament for Dorset, acting in 'the unavoidable absence of
the Earl of Shaftesbury' (*Dorset County Chronicle*, 27 August 1885), was connected by
marriage to the prominent Bankes family of Kingston Lacy. 'not far from 30',
'young . . . pouty', and 'given . . . Floyer' are late additions.

15.4   *The History . . . a Hand*: cf. 23.7–8, and especially TH's note, dated 19
February 1889, on 'The story of a face' at *LW* 226.

15.5   *A white frost*: cf. TH's reference to the Canadian 'silver frost' at *LN* i. 100.

15.7   *Froom Valley*: Lewell Mill was on the main channel of the River Froom (now
more commonly spelled Frome) at a point just east of Dorchester and quite close
to Max Gate, the house TH had built for himself and in which he lived from 1885
onwards.

15.10   *moving under enchantment*: cf. TH's note written after a May 1890 visit to the
Royal Academy: 'the curious effect upon an observer of the fashionable crowd—
seeming like people moving about under enchantment, or as somnambulists' (*LW*
235–6). As this 'Poetical Matter' entry suggests, TH did indeed 'often think' of
people acting without volition; see, e.g., his invocations of somnambulism at *LW*
190, 192, and *PN* 59 (the *PN* note is also included at *LW* 449). See also TH's ideas
for representing characters in *The Dynasts* detailed at *LW* 261 and especially at *LW*
211–12: 'Napoleon by means of necromancy becomes possessed of an insight
enabling him to see the thoughts of opposing generals'. Cf. 21.3–5. 'or somnambu-
lism.' and 'Also that makers . . . works.' are late additions.

16.1   *Souls gliding*: the 'great vault' refers to what was at that time the round
Reading Room of the British Museum. '[Entered M]': i.e., entered in 'Materials',
TH's term for the items collected for potential inclusion in the autobiographical
LW, where this note is indeed present (*LW* 215), differing in detail but essentially
the same. Absent from *LW*, however, is TH's apparent afterthought, 'Or souls of
the authors – midnight – '.

16.8–18   *Feb 24. 1888. . . . lived.*: written on a smaller faintly ruled sheet, evidently
extracted from one of TH's pocket-books, and pasted into 'Poetical Matter', where
it occupies approximately two-thirds of the page. The first two lines (from the date

to the first syllable of 'appeared') are written over a largely irrecoverable erasure. At some point, perhaps when pasting the note into 'Poetical Matter', TH evidently changed his mind about which names to represent in full: the recovery of all erasures in the note's second paragraph reveals that 'Sq—' was previously recorded as 'Squibb' and 'M....s' as 'Moors', but that 'Fuller' was entered merely as 'F—'.

Offering a rare if retrospective glimpse into the world in which TH grew up, the note is interestingly close in date to the 1 March 1888 note at *LW* 214–15 on the recollected 'village beauties' of the same period. TH's reference to 'Valentine hues' invokes the associations of St Valentine's day, just ten days earlier than the date of his note, and effectively emphasizes the affectionate coloration of his childhood memories. Francis Pitney Brouncker Martin owned the Kingston Maurward estate (including Higher Bockhampton) from 1844 to 1853, the central years of TH's childhood. For TH's relationship to Martin's wife, Julia Augusta Martin, towards the end of that period, see *BR* 48–50. Susan Squibb of Higher Bockhampton, aged 31 in the 1851 census, can be identified here, together with: Benjamin Barrett, a Lower Bockhampton blacksmith, and his wife Elizabeth; the Lower Bockhampton schoolmaster Thomas Fuller and his wife, both described as 'well-trained' at *LW* 23; Thomas Moors, son of James Moors, another local smith; and Eliza or Elizabeth Plowman, who ran the local dame school that TH may have briefly attended (see *BR* 44). Others in the list might be guessed at from the census returns for Higher and Lower Bockhampton, Stinsford, etc., but not confidently confirmed.

17.1 *London*: TH's surviving letters of March 1888 are consistently dated from the Savile Club, of which he had been a member since 1878, but a reference to 'the Temperance Hotel' at *LW* 215 suggests that he was actually staying at the West Central Hotel on Woburn Place, just north of Russell Square. '[Also M]' signals (cf. 16.7) the note's inclusion among the 'Materials' assembled for use in *LW*, where it duly appears (*LW* 215), with some variants.

17.6 *M. Aurelius*: Marcus Aurelius (121–80 CE), Roman Emperor 161–80. For TH's copy (Beinecke) of *The Thoughts of the Emperor M. Aurelius Antoninus*, presented to him by Horace Moule in 1865, see *BR* 84. Marcus Aurelius, adopted when young by the Emperor Antoninus Pius, subsequently married Pius's daughter Annia Galeria Faustina (d. 175), who bore him numerous children. The accusations of promiscuity brought against her (known as Faustina the Younger) and her mother (Faustina the Elder) are now generally believed to have been without foundation, but TH— probably influenced by Swinburne's 'Faustine' in the 1866 *Poems and Ballads* volume he so much admired (see *CL* ii. 158–9, *Studies, Specimens*, 49–51, 66, etc.)—seems to have adopted Faustina/Faustine (in this note he first wrote 'Faustine' and then altered the 'e' to an 'a') as a general term for women he perceived as dangerously attractive and sexually threatening: cf. 53.10, 65.11; *LW* 196, 221; and *Tess*, ch. 53 (*W* 472). There is also the moment in *The Well-Beloved*, II. xii, when Avice the Second, struggling to free herself from Pierston's embrace, knocks down his sculpture of 'the Empress Faustina's head' (*W* 132).

17.8 *The man of large mind*: TH's version of the trope of critical observer from elsewhere; cf. the New Zealander gazing on the ruins of London in Macaulay's 'Von Ranke' essay (1840), W. D. Howells's *A Traveller from Altruria* (1892–3), etc.

17.15 *Tragic drama*: no documented source for this anecdote has been discovered, and it may well be one of TH's invented 'satires of circumstance'.

18.3 *Extraordinary gale*: reports of an exceptionally strong gale along the English Channel ('In Dorsetshire a large number of trees have been uprooted, buildings blown down, and telegraph wires destroyed') appear in *The Times*, 14 Oct. 1891, 6.

18.6 *Pulling down houses*: 'f. p's' are evidently fireplaces.

18.7 <u>*The unknown ancestor*</u>: 'J. A.' is John Antell (1848–1935), TH's first cousin, son of his mother's sister Mary Hand and of John Antell, the remarkable Puddletown shoemaker (see 28.5 n. and 57.15–16 and n.). Mary Antell died on 28 November 1891, and TH probably wrote the original note after attending her funeral. Her grave in Puddletown churchyard has recently been built over and the tombstone re-erected some distance away.

18.14 *[Excision]*: approximately three-fifths of the leaf cut away at the bottom.

18.15 <u>*Lying listening*</u>: although TH seems not to have developed a poem from this particular note, he had of course invoked similar ideas in, e.g., 'Friends Beyond' (*CPW* i. 78–9), first published in *Wessex Poems* in 1898. Cf. 32.6–8 and 61.13–16. 'or at the service generally.' is a late addition.

18.17 *Samuel Wakely*: little is known about this eighteenth-century Dorset composer, but he seems to have been born in Swanage in 1705 and to have lived mostly in Bridport. His church music was certainly familiar to the Stinsford west-gallery musicians in the early decades of the nineteenth century. One of his psalm tunes is invoked in ch. 33 of *The Mayor of Casterbridge* (*W* 268), and the name of TH's grandfather ('T. Hardy, Bockington') appears among the subscribers to two collections of his church music, both printed in Bridport but undated. See also 32.3, *CL* iii. 286, and *PV* 323. 'travels . . . paper, &c' is a late addition.

19.2 *Shaded lamp*: a similarly worded note, also dated 13 September 1893, occurs at *LW* 275. TH must have inserted '(old)' as he was copying the note from its original source. In 1893 he was still occupying at Max Gate the study with windows to the west and north in which he had written *Tess of the d'Urbervilles*. From 1896 onwards he worked in the new east-facing study that had been built on to the back of the house. For illustrations of the two studies, see *BR* between pp. 244 and 245 and facing p. 372.

19.11 <u>*Ten tales*</u>: it seems likely that this had originally been an idea for a sequence of short prose narratives and that TH inserted '(in verse)' as he was transcribing.

19.15 <u>*Thunderstorm*</u>: the central section of this note ('white bull . . . struck dead.'), repeated with some wording differences at 32.9–12, evidently derives from a letter in which 'K.', TH's youngest sister Kate, described a thunderstorm experienced while she was teaching school in the north Dorset village of Sandford Orcas in the early 1880s. The 'additions'—presumably TH's own elaborations—are constituted by the opening clauses of the first complete sentence ('Before it came . . . livid –') and the fourth sentence ('The furze . . . snakes.'), both inscribed above the lines and marked for insertion. The phrase 'with additions' is itself a late addition.

20.10 *Poem entitled*: an entry clearly related to and perhaps prompted by its immediate predecessor. TH has evidently underlined what he thought the best of the possible titles. 'e.g. And did . . . been? &c' is a late addition.

21.3 *Conceive a person*: see 15.10–19 and n. As TH develops his idea, it seems to become closer to his presentation of Napoleon in *The Dynasts*.

21.12 *To-day*: this note appears at *LW* 302, dated 27 January 1897 and somewhat more crisply written.

21.15 *I cannot help noticing*: also included, slightly expanded, at *LW* 302.

21.17 *Passing Harris's*: Samuel Robert Harris was a fruiterer, nurseryman, seedsman, and florist, with a shop on Dorchester's High East Street and a nursery in adjoining Fordington. The 'decoration' itself (again described at 33.3–4) had evidently survived from some official occasion similar to, though more recent than, the 1849 visit of Prince Albert that TH drew upon in *The Mayor of Casterbridge* (see *BR* 231).

22.3 *"The Dancing Class"*: TH draws here upon two separate sources, the Weymouth dancing classes that he attended in the late 1860s (see *LW* 66) and the little business in baby goods conducted by Mrs Elizabeth Banger, an elderly Puddletown widow who died in 1842 but whose employees in her last years included Mary Hand, TH's aunt (later the wife of John Antell), and Absalom King, almost certainly to be identified with the A. King who acted as TH's godfather (see *BR* 43).

22.7 *P. Town ch. yd.*: the echoes in this note of TH's poem 'Voices from Things Growing in a Churchyard' (*CPW* ii. 395–7, *LW* 446–7), first published in December 1921 and subsequently collected in *Late Lyrics and Earlier* (1922), are in some respects developed in the immediately following notes. The specific reference here, however, is not to Stinsford but to Puddletown churchyard, where ancestors and relatives from both sides of TH's family were buried (cf. 18.7 n.). 'Weatherbury' is TH's name for Puddletown as fictionally evoked in *Far from the Madding Crowd* and elsewhere.

23.1 *Poem to Nature*: cf. 40.17–18 and 73.3–18. 'N's enquiry' is written over an erasure: 'N's Answr'.

23.7 *The Hand*: cf. 15.4.

23.9 *Man asleep*: '(end)' is a late addition. By '[Has this been written?]', TH clearly means written by himself. Although no such poem has been identified, 'Outside the Casement' (*CPW* ii. 443–4), first published in *Late Lyrics and Earlier* (1922), describes a similar dramatic situation.

23.13 *Another*: i.e., another poem.

23.17 *The tailor's shop*: no Dorchester tailoring or other business matching the initials 'G. D. & J.' has been identified, and TH could possibly have had a London firm in mind. That he wrote 'avoids growing' instead of 'avoids going' was perhaps the result of his thinking ahead to 'increasing', just two words further on.

24.10 *Local Names*: 'Yallm' is Yallam, a popular form of Yellowham (or Yell'ham) Hill, on the road from Dorchester to Puddletown, 'Blackn' is Black Down, the hill south-west of Dorchester where stands the monument to Admiral Sir Thomas Masterman Hardy of Trafalgar fame (cf. 33.5–9), and 'Wynyard's' is Wynyard's Gap, a hill-top cutting north-west of Maiden Newton. Holywell is a hamlet just south of the point where Benvill Lane crosses the main Dorchester to Yeovil road (Evershot railway station was and is located there); the gift of Holywell to Abbotsbury Abbey is recorded on a brass slab dating from c.1320 in the parish church of Askerswell. 'Banger's' has not survived as a name, but the wood itself, apparently planted by an eighteenth- or early nineteenth-century Thomas Banger (cf.

22.3 n.), was located on a higher part of the heath north-east of the Hardy cottage. 'Lulworth' is presumably to be identified with Bindon Hill, overlooking Lulworth Cove on the Dorset coast. Long Ash Lane was the contemporary name for the straight segment of the old Roman road running north from Grimstone to Holywell (cf. the opening paragraph of TH's 'Interlopers at the Knap'). 'Creech' refers to the section of the Purbeck Hills overlooking Creech Grange in south-east Dorset, due south of Wareham. Rainbarrows are a group of ancient tumuli, now much eroded, that stand on a high point of the heath overlooking the Frome valley and were prominently evoked in *The Return of the Native*, ch. 3 (*W* 15–17). A few of the actual names in this note also occur in TH's verse—e.g., in 'The Comet at Yell'ham' (*CPW* i. 188–9)—but he seems not to have used any of the suggested alternatives, except in so far as 'Sighing Hill' approximates to the 'Moaning Hill' of 'The Dead Quire' (*CPW* i. 310–14), dated 1897 and first published in 1901.

25.1   *A suffering God*: this note, partially echoed at 40.16–41.4 and 50.10–11, is repeated and identically dated at 72.15–73.2.

25.5   *Ezekiel*: in *Encyclopædia Biblica: A Critical Dictionary of the Literary, Political and Religious History, the Archæology, Geography and Natural History of the Bible*, ed. the Revd. T. K. Cheyne and J. Sutherland Black, 4 vols. (London: Adam and Charles Black, 1899–1903), ii., col. 1461, Ezekiel's visions are described as 'too elaborate for a moment of ecstasy—they are, in their present form, the product of careful study and composition . . . Ezekiel in these cases used the vision as a mere literary form.' A copy of a 1914 1-vol. edition of the *Encyclopædia Biblica* was in the Max Gate library. Other references to Cheyne are at *CL* iv. 47, vi. 374, and *LN* ii. 203; for TH's interest in the *Encyclopædia Biblica* during his final illness, see *LW* 479.

25.6   *Every box . . . memories*: broadly related to the poem 'Old Furniture' (*CPW* ii. 227–8), first published in *Moments of Vision* (1917).

25.7   *A wandering*: by 'marks & remains' TH evidently means archaeological evidence.

25.10   *Ballads by the Beldame*: despite the implicit allusion to line 46 of Milton's early poem 'At a Vacation Exercise in the College' ('When beldam Nature in her cradle was'), TH seems here to be invoking 'Beldame' less in the sense of ancestress than in that of malevolent old woman, hag, or witch.

25.17   *blooth*: a word also used by William Barnes and identified by *OED* as a southwestern dialect form of the obsolete 'blowth', meaning 'Blowing or blossoming; blossom, bloom'. Cf. *CL* vi. 76 and TH's use of 'bloothing' in the manuscript of 'The Temporary the All' and of 'apple-blooth', revised from 'blooth', in 'The Dance at the Phœnix' (*CPW* i. 7, 57); both poems were first published in *Wessex Poems*.

26.4   *Wet night*: Grey's Bridge, the eighteenth-century stone bridge over the River Frome on the main road just east of Dorchester, is implicitly invoked as the further out of the two bridges in *The Mayor of Casterbridge*, ch. 32. The Bow, the curved street wall of St Peter's Church, is at the centre of Dorchester, uphill from Grey's Bridge. For TH's fascination with the effects of light (as in 'Road shone'), see 8.1 n.

26.7   *Reminiscences by Destiny*: retrospectively added, as was the capitalization, emphasized by double underlining, of the two occurrences of 'it'. Both the date and the content of this note suggest a close association with *The Dynasts*, of which the first volume appeared early in 1904. In a 1907 letter on the philosophy of *The Dynasts*, TH wrote: 'That the Unconscious Will of the Universe is growing aware of Itself I believe I may claim as my own idea solely—at which I arrived by reflecting that what has already taken place in fractions of the Whole (i.e. so much of the world as has become conscious) is likely to take place in the Mass; & there being no Will outside the Mass—that is, the Universe—the whole Will becomes conscious thereby; & ultimately, it is to be hoped, sympathetic. I believe too, that the Prime Cause, this Will, has never before been called It, in any literature English or foreign' (*CL* iii. 255; see also *LW* 360–1). Cf. 'A Philosophical Fantasy', first published 1 January 1927 and subsequently collected in *Winter Words* (*CPW* iii. 234–8, 344–51, and see 41.1 n.).

26.11–13   ~~O Time . . . &c.~~: as Taylor has noted (*Language*, 310), these initial jottings finally emerged, totally rewritten, as 'Thoughts at Midnight' (*CPW* iii. 168–9), first published in *Winter Words*. This note, the struck-through note at 37.2–5, and the recoverable erased notes (see 4.13 n. and 6.8 n.) jointly provide a rare opportunity for analysing TH's creative processes: see Introduction. As of 25 May 1906 TH had just been reading J. McT. E. McTaggart's recently published *Some Dogmas of Religion*: see *CL* iii. 207–8 and *LW* 317.

26.14   *Isochronism*: TH's source was Coventry Patmore's 'Prefatory Study on English Metrical Law'—revised from an essay in the *North British Review* 27 (Aug. 1857), 127–61—as prefixed to his *Amelia, Tamerton Church-Tower, Etc.* (London: George Bell & Sons, 1878), 3–85. TH's extracts, however, are frequently abridged and/or paraphrased, and he juxtaposes passages that in the original are quite widely separated: see, in succession, Patmore's pages 33–4, 50, 53, 82–3, 83, and 83–4. Although the final question mark within parentheses evidently relates to the idea being propounded rather than to the accuracy of the transcription, TH does not altogether reflect Patmore's emphasis in the sentence overall: 'Such variety must be incessantly inspired by, and expressive of, ever-varying emotion' (p. 84). TH's interest in questions of equality in metrical length raised by Patmore's discussion of 'isochronism' (literally 'equal-timeness') is further indicated by the inclusion of extensive notes from this same source in 'Literary Notes II' (*LN* ii. 190–2). See also Taylor, *Metres*, esp. 18–28, 60–3.

27.4   *A white smocked shepherd*: cf. the shepherd 'in a white smock-frock' counting his sheep in 'An Unkindly May' (*CPW* iii. 174); see 6.8 n.

27.5   *The voice . . . palpitates in*: a quotation from an unsigned review, 'Modern Developements in Ballad Art', *Edinburgh Review*, 213 (Jan. 1911), 153–79: '[N]o modern imaginative faculty can effectually reproduce the actuality of the centuries of faith when they indited their ballads of supernatural adventure. The voice of fear palpitates in the verses that tell of the spectres of the Wild Hunt; of lovers revenant whose dead lips kiss with the scent of the mould on them; . . .' (p. 158).

27.8   *The Persistence*: the term 'The Unknowable' (i.e., the force that drives the universe) provides the title of Part I of Herbert Spencer's *First Principles* (London: Williams & Norgate, 1862) and recurs on numerous occasions throughout that work. TH owned two copies of *First Principles*, an extensively marked 'Fourth Edition' of 1880 and a two-volume 'Popular Edition' of 1910 (both in the Harry Ransom Center, University of Texas at Austin). In 1893 he referred to it as 'a book which acts, or used to act, upon me as a sort of patent expander when I had been particularly narrowed down by the events of life. Whether the theories are true or false, their effect upon the imagination is unquestionable, and I think beneficial' (*CL* ii. 24–5). See also *LW* 400; *LN* i. 335–6, ii. 108, 153, 457, 557; and Taylor, *Language*, 263–4. TH in this note appears to be absorbing Spencer's term into his own conception of 'the Will' as elaborated in *The Dynasts*, itself invoked in the next note.

27.10   *An Epic-Drama*: as originally written on 29 May 1914, this note constituted an ironic if unconscious anticipation of the world-wide disaster of the First World War that would begin just 2 months later. Cf. the poem 'Channel Firing' (*CPW* ii. 9–10), first published 1 May 1914, that TH in retrospect referred to as 'prophetic' (*LW* 394).

27.14   *The "Fly" view*: cf. the similar note at 39.2–4, where the 'old note-book' appears to be more directly quoted; see also 53.15–54.8 and n.

27.15   *The Ibsen manner*: TH's summary of a review of Ibsen's *Ghosts* at the Kingsway Theatre, London, published in *The Times*, 30 Apr. 1917. The anonymous reviewer compared *Ghosts* to the *Œdipus Tyrannus* as demonstrating 'the tragic crisis of a story which you are bidden to put together piecemeal by retrospection' (p. 11).

28.3   *H. Irving*: '(See 2 leaves on)' is an interlinear addition, presumably added after TH created the more extensive Irving note at 29.5–17. For other references to 'The Wife of Usher's Well', see 3.20 and 14.7–8.

28.5   *Self "hideously multiplied"*: the quotation is from Shelley's *The Revolt of Islam*, Canto Third, stanza 23: 'All shapes like mine own self hideously multiplied'; cf. *Jude the Obscure*, Part Fifth, ch. 4 (*W* 345). 'Gen! S.' is presumably General Sir Horatio Shirley (1805–79; *OxfordDNB*), brother of the Revd Arthur Shirley, vicar of Stinsford, and 'J.A.' must be TH's uncle John Antell (1816–78), the Puddletown shoemaker on whom Jude Fawley in *Jude the Obscure* may have been partly based (see 57.15–16 and n.). Both men lived in Puddletown, and, despite the wide difference in social class, they would at least have known each other by sight. The precise application of the Shelley quotation remains unclear—to judge from their photographs in *Thomas Hardy Annual No. 2* (London: Macmillan, 1984), 174, and *BR*, following p. 116, the two men did not greatly resemble each other—but they may have suffered from similar indispositions, and it would in any case appear that on perhaps more than one occasion the upper-class Shirley, proceeding uphill in his carriage, had driven past the radical John Antell, toiling up on foot, without offering him a ride.

28.10   *Epitaphs*: the date of July 1915 appended to this list of Shakespearian epitaphs seems to rule out their having been occasioned by the death at Gallipoli in late August 1915 of TH's distant but much admired cousin Frank George (see *LW* 401, *PV* 361–2, and *BR* 464, 465). One possibility is that they were prompted by the July 1915 suicide and Stinsford burial of TH's friend Douglas Thornton, a local banker who had lived at Birkin House, not far from Stinsford church. References for the quotations are given in sequence as follows: *Much Ado About Nothing*, i. i. 311; *Comedy of Errors*, i. i. 137; *Hamlet*, iv. v. 175; *Antony and Cleopatra*, v. ii. 119; *Cymbeline*, iii. i. 2–3; *Measure for Measure*, v. i. 426; *Much Ado About Nothing*, iii. i. 47–8.

28.18–29.1   *There are two . . . transmission*: TH, a vice-president of the English Association, appears to be summarizing (without actually quoting) a portion of 'On

Playing the Sedulous Ape', an essay by George Sampson (1873–1950; *OxfordDNB*), teacher and literary scholar, as originally published in the Association's *Essays and Studies*, VI (1920): 'In the mind of the artist there is laid up, as a sort of Platonic ideal, the "something" as "something said"; and his trouble is to get that "something said" from his mind to his paper with the least diminution of its original brightness' (pp. 76–7).

29.3–4   *'all the charm . . . word.'*: a periodical cutting somewhat laboriously reconstructed from three separate pieces which had been pasted into an earlier ruled notebook—perhaps one of TH's pocket-books—prior to being cut out and inserted in 'Poetical Matter'. The lines themselves are slightly misquoted from the third stanza of Tennyson's 'To Virgil' ('All the charm of all the Muses | often flowering in a lonely word'), and TH's failure to recognize their source is somewhat surprising in light of his evident familiarity with Tennyson's work.

29.5   *Addenda*: i.e., additional to the brief note at 28.3. Sir Henry Irving (1838–1905; *OxfordDNB*), the most famous actor of his day, turned down the stage version of *The Woodlanders* when it was offered to him in 1891 (Irving to TH, 28 Apr. 1891, DCM), but he and TH were nevertheless on friendly terms (see *LW* 349). When Irving collapsed and died on 13 October 1905 after playing the leading role in a performance of Tennyson's *Becket*, TH perceived the irony of the famous actor's being simultaneously reported as dead on p. 9 of *The Times* of 14 October (in the day's 'Contents' column, with a cross-reference to the actual obituary on p. 6) and listed on the facing p. 8 (among the theatrical advertisements) as about to perform at the Theatre Royal, Bradford, that same evening. Since pp. 8 and 9 were the newspaper's attached centre pages and only one column of text (plus the intervening gutter) separated the two announcements—the death notice appearing in the first column of p. 9, the theatrical notice in the fifth (of six columns) of p. 8— TH was able to cut both announcements out as a single extract, which he then pasted onto a slip of paper that was itself pasted into 'Poetical Matter' at some subsequent point. (That the slip had been clipped together with other pieces of paper before being detached for insertion in the notebook is suggested by a tear in its left margin.) TH's explanatory sentence, '(It . . . 1905.)', appears on an otherwise blank segment of this same slip. As thus inserted, the text from p. 9 extended beyond the right-hand side of the notebook page, but was evidently capable of being folded back over the performance announcement. Not reproduced here are the accompanying printed texts from pp. 8 and 9 (the latter texts crossed through, the former not) that TH preserved in order to contextualize the ironic contiguity of the two announcements. The underlining in both announcements is TH's.

30.1   *1882. Snow*: the references are to the French victory over the Austrians and Bavarians at Hohenlinden, near Munich, on 3 December 1800; Napoleon's disastrous winter retreat from Moscow in 1812; and the fatal entrapment of Sir John Franklin's ships in thick ice while searching for the North-West Passage in 1845–8. Cf. *LW* 163, for a TH note on the severe winter weather of December 1882.

30.7   *"The Sceptic's Doom"*: an idea perhaps related at some level to TH's own devotion to the liturgy and music of the Church of England; cf. the 1883 note at *LW* 167: 'Poetry versus reason: e.g., . . . a hymn rolls from a church-window, and the uncompromising No-God-ist or Unconscious-God-ist takes up the refrain.' Coleridge's 'The Rime of the Ancient Mariner' is again invoked at 40.6.

30.12   *Ewelease Stile*: situated at the point, near Kingston Maurward House, where the path from Higher Bockhampton across a broad sheep pasture ('ewelease' or 'eweleaze') met the Dorchester to Tincleton road. TH would twice daily have climbed over that stile during his Dorchester schooldays, and during the early stages of his architectural apprenticeship it was evidently here, roughly half-way between Dorchester and Higher Bockhampton, that he met and talked with his intensely religious (Baptist) colleague Henry Bastow, who subsequently emigrated to Australia. That the spot had still other associations for TH is suggested by the entry at *LW* 450, by the drawings accompanying 'Her Immortality' and 'In a Eweleaze near Weatherbury' in the first (1898) edition of *Wessex Poems* (*CPW* i. 74, 92), and by his identification of 'Kingston-Maurward Ewelease' as the setting for 'An Anniversary' (*CPW* ii. 209–10), first published in *Moments of Vision*.

30.13   *Ballads*: the shorthand or other symbol preceding 'Ballads' has not been deciphered. The quotation is from the traditional ballad 'Sweet William's Ghost' (Child ballad 77; see stanza 12 of version A or B).

30.15   *Allan Water*: the well-known song, 'The Banks of Allan Water', written by M. G. Lewis, seems originally to have been sung to a variety of traditional tunes; increasingly, however, it was sung to just one tune that itself became—and remains—known as 'The Banks of Allan Water'. The song provided TH with the line 'And a winning tongue had he', quoted in ch. 23 of *Far from the Madding Crowd* (*W* 179) and proposed at one point as the title for the novel that became *A Pair of Blue Eyes* (*CL* i. 17).

30.16   *Oct 1888*: given the approximate character of TH's dating here, it seems feasible to associate this note with the walk from Evershot station (located at Holywell: see 24.10 n.) that he specifically dated 30 September 1888 (*LW* 223–4). The possible relevance of both walk and mistletoe to ch. 35 of *Tess of the d'Urbervilles* (*W* 299), the novel on which TH was then working, is explored at *BR* 270–1.

32.3   *Sam⸍ Wakeley*: see 18.17 (and n.), where the name is correctly spelled Wakely.

32.5   *[Excision]*: approximately a quarter of the leaf cut away at the top.

32.7   *On a Christmas Day*: evidently an idea for a nostalgic poem invoking the three members of TH's family who had formerly played together in the old west gallery choir and now lay buried in Stinsford churchyard: TH's father (1811–92), just recently deceased, his grandfather (1778–1837), and his uncle James (1805–80). Cf. 18.15–16 and n.

32.9   *Scene at Sandford Orcas*: an unexpanded version of the entry at 19.15–20.2. The basic note (here the last three sentences) is present in both entries, though with minor textual divergences such as often appear in TH's transcriptions, whether from haste, carelessness, or an initial shaping of the material for creative purposes.

33.3   *At Harris's*: cf. the similar though evidently separate note on Harris's nursery at 21.17–22.2.

33.5   *Black'on Monument*: monument on Black Down hill, south-west of Dorchester (cf. 24.12), commemorating Admiral Sir Thomas Masterman Hardy, Nelson's flag-captain at the Battle of Trafalgar, who was perhaps remotely connected to TH (see *CL* iii. 234–5, 260). TH's companions on the expedition were ELH and her nephew Gordon Gifford, who was currently staying at Max Gate while receiving architectural training from TH (see *CL* ii. 245).

33.15 *utilitarianism of Mill*: TH admired John Stuart Mill (1806–73; *Oxford DNB*), both as author and as thinker, and was much impressed by his one glimpse of Mill on the hustings in the 1860s (*PV* 238–9). In addition to an 1867 edition of Mill's *On Liberty* (DCM) he owned a copy of the 5th (1874) edition of *Utilitarianism* (Beinecke) and quoted three passages from it in *The Hand of Ethelberta*, ch. 36 (*W* 318–19).

33.16 *[Excision]*: approximately a quarter of the leaf cut away at the bottom.

33.17 *1872. My.*: at this date TH's sister Mary was teaching in Piddlehinton (see 13.3 n.). The Mayo family worked Little Piddle Farm nearby, and 'old Mayo' was presumably the recently deceased George Mayo, whose tomb in the village church-yard gives his death date as 1872.

34.9 *[Erasure]*: the original four-line note is essentially irrecoverable.

34.14 *Aug 26. 1868*: the earliest dated note in 'Poetical Matter' (for the earliest dated entry, see 76.1–79.5). Interestingly reflective of TH's sexual susceptibilities, the note belongs to the period he spent back at Higher Bockhampton following his departure from London because of ill health in the summer of 1867 and was writ-ten shortly after the arrival of Alexander Macmillan's remarkable letter about *The Poor Man and the Lady* (*LW* 59–60, *BR* 102–3). Lulworth Cove is a horseshoe-shaped cliff-surrounded bay on the south Dorset coast some 10 miles east of Weymouth that TH incorporated in *Far from the Madding Crowd* as Lulwind Cove, the location of Troy's supposed drowning. TH's poem 'The Maid of Keinton Mandeville' (*CPW* ii. 326–7), recalling a young woman who sang at a Sturminster Newton concert in 1878 (*LW* 122, *BR* 179–80), was first published in April 1920 and subsequently col-lected in *Late Lyrics and Earlier* (1922). It is unclear whether the reference in the concluding parenthetical suggestion is to the 'Maid' herself, as one of the subjects of a possible poem about attractive women glimpsed but not known, or to the inclu-sion of the existing poem within a 'Women seen' sequence of poems. If the latter, the absence of such a sequence from *Late Lyrics* would seem to indicate that TH's suggestion, integral to the note as included in 'Poetical Matter', was incorporated at some point between the writing of the poem and the publication of *Late Lyrics*.

36.4 *(? 1880–1920.)*: TH's initial question mark evidently reflects some uncer-tainty as to precisely when he first arrived at the philosophical view represented in this diagram, but the presence below '1880' of an irrecoverable erased date fol-lowed by a full stop seems to indicate his having dated the diagram itself by the year in which he first designed it—probably during the period (*c.*1900–7) when he was writing *The Dynasts*. Represented by the diagram is TH's belief, sustained beyond the indicated terminal date of 1920, that the 'Prime Force or Forces'—convention-ally defined as 'God' but more commonly referred to by TH as the Will, the Cause of Things, or the Invariable Antecedent (see *LW* 235, 406, etc.)—was in fact uncon-scious, 'neither moral nor immoral, but *un*moral', as he wrote in December 1920 (*CL* vi. 54, *LW* 439), hence essentially 'Neutral'. TH on the one hand categorically rejected the notion of the Prime Force as 'Maleficent', while on the other his acute identification with the world's suffering rendered him incapable of belief in a 'Beneficent' (orthodox Christian) 'God'. Even so, his idea that the Unconscious Will was evolving, gradually becoming conscious and 'ultimately, it is to be hoped, sympathetic' (*CL* iii. 255), implies a belief that the Cause of Things had at least the potential to become a beneficent force; cf. 26.7 n. TH's training as an architect had of course accustomed him to the use of the pencil, and other instances of his diagrammatic representations of abstract ideas include the charts and diagrams of human psychology, dated 1863, that he inscribed on the recto and verso of a leaf tipped into 'Literary Notes I', and the less elaborate drawings in the same notebook of Comte's theories of the human brain and of social progress (*LN* i. 3–4, 74, 76, and 239–40).

36.11   *Mth*   Tenderness: 'Mth' (for 'Method')—here and at 41.11—indicates TH's deliberate analysis of the specific ways in which particular poetical effects are created. The quotation, seen by TH as successfully evoking tenderness, is from a poem entitled 'Change'; it is inserted in the form of a cutting from a review in *The Nation and Athenæum*, 30 Oct. 1926, 150, of Mary Stella Edwards's *Time and Chance: Poems*, published by Leonard and Virginia Woolf at the Hogarth Press, 1926. The book, together with its price and publication details, is also mentioned in the 'Memoranda II' notebook (see *PN* 94), and is perhaps to be associated with the Woolfs' July 1926 visit to Max Gate (*BR* 523–4), although its absence from the reconstruction of the contents of the Max Gate library suggests that TH did not go so far as to purchase it.

Because this note, at the top of an otherwise excised leaf, was not written over an erasure, it would appear to indicate that by late October or early November 1926 TH had already reached this point in the notebook, and that all the subsequent entries were made between that date and mid-December 1927, the last working months of his life. The note seems in any case to reflect, within 'Poetical Matter' as a whole, a shift of emphasis and concern away from copying old notes and in the direction of thinking more deliberately about poetry and poetic methods, formulating new ideas, glimpsing new possibilities, and occasionally experimenting with verse drafts. It may even mark a moment when TH, with *Winter Words* clearly in view, returned to the notebook after not having used it for some period of time.

37.1   *[Excision]*: approximately two-thirds of leaf cut away at bottom.

37.2   *The party at W. P. V.*: 'W. P. V.' stands for Westbourne Park Villas, where (at no. 16) TH lodged from mid-1863 to mid-1867, four of the five years he spent working in London as an assistant architect; 'the quadrilles' evidently emerged from his memories of a party and its music overheard at that distant time. Because this note, like that at 26.11–13, has been struck through rather than excised or erased beyond recovery, it provides a rare opportunity for analysing TH's development of an initial 'given' into a dramatic—and characteristically ironic—situation capable of eventual realization as the poem 'In the Marquee' (*CPW* iii. 211–12), first collected in *Winter Words* following prior publication in the *Daily Telegraph* (Purdy, 261). The comment on the poem in Purdy (p. 256) was based on this note. For *Winter Words* poems originating in erased 'Poetical Matter' notes, see 4.13 n. and 6.8 n. 'P. T. Gate' is the Puddletown turnpike gate, formerly located across the main road just outside the village itself.

37.6   *Cerne Abbey*: TH was always interested in the few visible remains of the Abbey that once stood in the mid-Dorset village of Cerne Abbas (see 40.2–15, *PV* 171–2, and *CL* ii. 270). The source of his reference to the apostate monks is correctly identified as Hutchins, iv. 23, and there is a pencil line alongside this passage in TH's own copy of Hutchins (DCM). '[because he was unworthy?]' is a late addition.

37.10   *A man goes*: TH explores somewhat similar ideas in, e.g., 'The Dead Man Walking' (*CPW* i. 267–8).

37.12–15   *There is nae Covenant . . . through*: TH quotes, accurately, the opening lines of 'The Covenanter's Lament', written by the Scottish poet Robert Allan (1774–1841) and published in his *Evening Hours: Poems and Songs* (Glasgow: David Robertson, etc., 1836), 69–70. It could be sung to an air called 'The Martyr's Grave'.

37.16   *Verse one*: marked with TH's shorthand symbol for 'poem', this entry should clearly be read as the draft opening of the potential verse dialogue that is picked up again in the following entry. The two entries are, however, separated by a largely irrecoverable erasure (see next annotation) and it is not clear to what extent TH had drafted the intervening stages of the dialogue.

37.17   *[Erasure]*: the original entries—comprising five double-column lines of verse squeezed into the top margin and next one and a half lines, followed by five lines of prose—are largely irrecoverable. The erased '1' and '2' heading the verse columns do, however, indicate that the verse lines were a continuation of the verse draft begun on the preceding notebook page (i.e., 37.16).

38.3   *Nature's ignorance*: cf. 25.10–12, 73.13–18, and esp. TH's letter, headed 'M. Maeterlinck's Apology for Nature', in the *Academy and Literature*, 17 May 1902 (*PV* 174–6).

38.10   *A thousand . . . day*: 'But, beloved, be not ignorant of this one thing, that one day is with the Lord as a thousand years, and a thousand years as one day' (2 Pet. 3: 8). 'something as Knight's' refers to the moment in *A Pair of Blue Eyes* (ch. 22) when Knight stared at a fossil in the cliff-face to which he was clinging and 'Time closed up like a fan before him' (*W* 242); cf. 65.5–6.

38.12   *Childe Harold*: the widely travelling and distinctly 'Byronic' central figure of Byron's long poem *Childe Harold's Pilgrimage*. A somewhat similar idea of a person living 'through the centuries' appears in the 'Memoranda II' notebook (*PN* 69) and at *LW* 452, in both instances dated 26 February 1923, identified as copied from 'an old note', and specifically defined as for 'A story (rather than a poem)'. The 'innocent vision' of Adam has obvious biblical roots but seems not to have been an actual quotation.

38.15   *The Via Sacra*: the main street of the ancient Forum in Rome, visited by TH and ELH (*LW* 195–9) while they were in Italy in 1887. Horace's *Satires* i. 9, which speaks of the poet's walking on the Via Sacra, is also alluded to at *LW* 198.

38.16   *The Sailors*: TH and ELH, visiting the Palazzo Ducale in Venice (*LW* 200), were viewing, along with some sailors, the large eighteenth-century revolving globe of the terrestrial sphere that can still be seen, together with a similar celestial sphere, in the Palazzo's 'Sala dello Scudo' (Shield Room).

39.1   *the Venus*: a plaster cast of the Venus de Milo, 2 feet 10 inches in height, was listed as Lot 145 in the sale of the Max Gate contents held in Dorchester on 16 February 1938, following FEH's death. TH and ELH had evidently purchased the figure during their Italian trip and arranged for it to be shipped to Max Gate, and it can be seen, reflected in a mirror, in a photograph of the drawing-room dating from about 1900. For a visitor's comment, see *TH Remembered*, 178. The actual Venus de Milo statue was first discovered in 1820.

39.2   *A room . . . skirting*: cf. the note from the year 1891 at *LW* 246: 'In the Gallery of the English Art Club: "If I were a painter I would paint a picture of a room as viewed by a mouse from a chink under the skirting."' The viewpoint of a fly is invoked at 27.14 and 53.15–16, and that of a watching bird in two story outlines (DCM) apparently written out by TH for possible completion and publication by Florence Dugdale, later FEH. See TH, 'Plots for Five Unpublished Short Stories', ed. Evelyn Hardy, in *The London Magazine*, 5.11 (Nov. 1958), 33–45.

39.5   *[Excision]*: approximately three-fifths of the leaf cut away at the bottom.

39.6   <u>*Why Orion*</u>: not in itself a new idea for TH, but it leads here to an interesting indication of his literary heroes.

39.12   *Ghosts at old Mad House*: the Pauper Lunatic Asylum built in 1832 as an extension to Forston House in Charminster (just north of Dorchester) was pulled down at some point following completion of the still existing Herrison Hospital in the 1860s: see John Newman and Nikolaus Pevsner, *The Buildings of England: Dorset* (Harmondsworth: Penguin Books, 1972), 143.

40.2   *Cerne Abbey*: for the Abbey and 'The Four Apostates', see 37.6–9 and n. For another reference to Coleridge's 'The Rime of the Ancient Mariner', see 30.10. 'Cerne Abbey cont<u>d</u>' was added by TH at the top of a new page to indicate that the immediately following notes belonged with those on the preceding page.

40.10   *Abbey field*: the field containing the remaining Abbey ruins was given over (as now) to the grazing of cattle. No 'William Beyminster' is named in Hutchins; TH presumably had in mind Roger Bemynster, elected abbot in 1470 (Hutchins, iv. 23). For TH's persistent hope that 'Some new enthusiasm' would lead to the reform and consequent re-energizing of the Church of England, see Dalziel, '"The Hard Case of the Would-be-Religious": Hardy and the Church from Early Life to Later Years', forthcoming in *A Companion to Thomas Hardy*, ed. Keith Wilson (Oxford: Blackwell Publishing).

40.16   *"God" poem, or poems*: the first of two sequences of notes for poems about 'God'; cf. the second sequence at 50.1–17. 'Poetical Matter' also includes individual 'God' notes at 25.1–4 (repeated at 72.15–73.2), 26.7–10, 36.4–10, and 72.1–5 (a partial repetition of 50.2–9).

40.17   *Not asking help*: this idea is developed in a verse draft and further prose note at 73.3–18.

41.1   *God deplores*: this idea was partly developed in 'A Philosophical Fantasy' (*CPW* iii. 234–8, 344–51), dated '1920 and 1926', first published 1 January 1927, and subsequently collected in *Winter Words* (see also *LW* 470). Cf. 26.7–10 and n.

41.3   *Hartm<u>n</u> II. 366*: the reference is to William Chatterton Coupland's 3-vol. English translation of Eduard von Hartmann's *Philosophy of the Unconscious*, first published in London by Trübner & Co. in 1884 and subsequently reprinted. TH's copy, an 1893 printing of the same 3-vol. edition, was sold as Lot 26 in the 1938 Hodgson sale of his library, and its present location is unknown. Numerous references to Coupland's translation appear in TH's literary notebooks (see *LN* i. 185, 395, ii. 109–14), and Hartmann is generally acknowledged to have been an important source for the philosophical ideas embodied in *The Dynasts*; see *TH Remembered*, 35, and Walter F. Wright, *The Shaping of 'The Dynasts': A Study in Thomas Hardy* (Lincoln, NB: University of Nebraska Press, 1967), esp. 47–55. At this point

in 'Poetical Matter' TH appears to be referring back not so much to Hartmann's
ii. 366 itself, as to his own part-quotation, part-summary, part-elaboration of the
relevant passage in 'Literary Notes II': 'If happ^{ss} be the end, there can only be
such sufferings as are unavoidable to attain on another side, or in a later stage,
higher happ^{ss}, or to obviate more extensive sufferings . . . otherwise it [God] w^d be
only driving the teeth into one's own [his own] flesh' (*LN* ii. 112; TH's ellipsis and
square brackets).

41.4   *Cf. Spinoza*: the occasional references to the Dutch philosopher Baruch Spin-
oza (1632–77) in TH's literary notebooks are sometimes taken from what TH calls
an 'excellent article' by Emanuel Deutsch in the 1892 edition of *Chambers's Ency-
clopaedia* (*LN* ii. 239; see also *LN* ii. 108–9, 238) and—despite the references in ch. 16
of *The Woodlanders* (*W* 138) and at *LW* 364—his acquaintance with Spinoza may
not have gone much further. Relevant here is a note (from *Chambers's*), which reads
in part: 'yet Spinoza's God neither thinks nor creates. . . . Everything visible is a
Mode of God's attribute of extension. God is the "immanent idea," the One & All,
the <u>natura</u> <u>naturans</u>; World, <u>natura</u> <u>naturata</u>, is one complex whole' (*LN* ii. 238;
TH's ellipsis).

41.11   <u>Mth</u>. *Sting in the tail*: 'Mth.', for 'Method' (cf. 36.11), indicates TH's appre-
ciation of the unexpected conclusion to the passage from the sixth verse paragraph
of Robert Buchanan's 'Penelope', first published in Buchanan's *Undertones* (1863)
but represented here by a pasted-in cutting, poorly printed and erroneously
punctuated, from an unlocated source. The marginal rule, 'by R. Buchanan.', and
the underlining of the concluding line are in TH's hand. The same lines of verse,
with the last line similarly emphasized, also appear in a cutting from a *Daily Chron-
icle* review of Archibald Stodart-Walker's *Robert Buchanan: The Poet of Modern Revolt.
An Introduction to His Poetry* (London: Grant Richards, 1901) that TH inserted in
'Literary Notes II' (see *LN* ii. 116, 522).

42.8   *an impression picture*: for TH's familiarity with and response to contemporary
Impressionist paintings and techniques, see Bullen, 181–2. See also *LW* 191, and
TH's use of the term 'impression-picture' in ch. 2 of *The Woodlanders* (*W* 9). '(for
process, not for titles)' and '(from notes of about 1900)' are late additions.

42.13   *Schleirmacher's*: so spelled by TH. Friedrich Schleiermacher (1768–1834),
the German theologian and philosopher, was an important figure in the develop-
ment of modern Protestant theology. Given the misspelling of Schleiermacher's
name, however, and the absence of his writings from the Max Gate library, it seems
likely that TH knew of his ideas only at second-hand. TH did own and mark a copy
(Beinecke) of the standard translation of Friedrich Ueberweg's *A History of Philo-
sophy. From Thales to the Present Time*, 2 vols. (London: Hodder & Stoughton, 1880),
and the reference there (ii. 254) to Schleiermacher's list of the cardinal virtues is
closely echoed in ch. 19 of *The Woodlanders* (*W* 167)—and more closely still in the
original manuscript of that novel (DCM).
  TH originally wrote and then erased the opening nine words of this note, cre-
ating a space between it and the preceding note and continuing with the reference
to Schleiermacher. 'What is it to <u>me</u>?'—just possibly an echo of Matt. 27: 4—evi-
dently refers back directly to the preceding note, while the second passage within
quotation marks seems not to be an actual quotation but rather TH's own attempt

to capture the essence of Schleiermacher's thought as presented by Ueberweg: e.g., 'with [Schleiermacher] space, time, and causality are not merely forms of a phenomenal world existing solely in the consciousness of the percipient Subject, but are also forms of the objective, real world which confronts him and conditions his knowledge' (ii. 244).

42.16   *As in "Desperate Remedies"*: see *Desperate Remedies*, VI. 2 (*W* 97–9).

43.1   *Songs} of Ignorance*: an obvious reference to William Blake's titles, *Songs of Innocence* and *Songs of Experience*.

43.3   *Gr—y's old one*: evidently a table in the Higher Bockhampton cottage that had belonged to TH's 'Granny', i.e., his father's mother, born Mary Head (1772–1857), whom TH affectionately remembered in the poems 'One We Knew' (*CPW* i. 331–2), first published in 1903 and subsequently collected in *Time's Laughingstocks* in 1909, and 'Domicilium' (*CPW* iii. 279–80, *LW* 8–9), first published in 1916.

43.4   *on a card table*: cf. 'The Autobiography of a Card Table' proposed in the 'Memoranda I' notebook (*PN* 25) and dated 1883. 'loq.' is an abbreviation for the Latin 'loquitur', hence 'the table speaks'.

43.5   *Marie Hamilton's*: TH quotes with essential accuracy the first stanza of the ballad 'Marie Hamilton' or 'The Queen's Marie' as it appears in his copy (DCM) of *The Ballad Minstrelsy of Scotland: Romantic and Historical*, 2nd edn. (Glasgow: Maurice Ogle, n.d. [*c*. 1871]), 511. Cf. Taylor, *Metres*, 211. This note is repeated essentially word for word at 70.1–5, and the ballad's narrative method is also invoked at 55.19.

43.8   *Scenes requiring keys*: the reference here is to 'Art. The Mixture as Before', a review of an exhibition at the New Gallery, London, that appeared over the initials C. L. H. (Charles Lewis Hind) in *Academy and Literature*, 62 (3 May 1902), 463–4, a dozen pages further on from the review of Maeterlinck's *The Buried Temple* that prompted the response from TH published in the 17 May issue of the same journal (*PV* 174–6). TH's immediate source, however, was perhaps the somewhat more detailed note included in 'Literary Notes II' (*LN* ii. 125), and he may never have seen the actual painting, 'Le Secret-Reflet', by the Belgian symbolist Fernand Khnopff (1858–1921). For a reproduction and discussion, see Lynne Pudles, 'Fernand Khnopff, Georges Rodenbach, and Bruges, the Dead City', *Art Bulletin*, 74.4 (Dec. 1992), 648–9.

43.10   *From a very old note: about 1905* – : retrospectively squeezed in above the line. At the conclusion of this note, squeezed into the bottom margin, is TH's direction to 'see on back' of the leaf, where at the bottom of the page he has written out his proposed metrical scheme for these poems. The quatrain opens with the first two lines of long measure (i.e., iambic tetrameter quatrains, sometimes using, as here, an *aabb* rhyme scheme), the form of some of TH's favourite hymns, including 'Awake, My Soul'. TH's third and the first of his fourth lines are derived from common song measure (i.e., anapaestic tetrameter quatrains, rhyming *aabb*). Cf. Taylor, *Metres*, 220–1.

44.7–8   *i.e., whittle . . . moment of it.*: a late addition.

44.14   *Place lyrics*: Sturminster Newton, Wimborne, and Boscastle were all important locations for TH in his relationship with ELH, and Enfield was the home town of Florence Dugdale, whom TH married in 1914 following ELH's death in November 1912. The Earl's Court Exhibition in west London, on the other hand, seems to have been mentioned by TH only once, in a letter of 13 April 1900 (*CL* ii. 254), as the location of a Woman's Exhibition that would include the portrait of himself painted by Winifred Thomson, with whom he had a genuine but not a romantic friendship. But while there is no specific evidence of his having visited the Earl's Court Exhibition site itself, it is possible to speculate that it was associated with an important moment in his relationship with Florence Dugdale. He was evidently spending time with her during the week-long visit he made to London without ELH between 6 and 13 July 1912 (*CL* iv. 223–4), and they could have gone together—she in her occasional capacity as a reporter for *The Standard* newspaper—to the elaborate pseudo-Elizabethan tournament staged at Earl's Court during the evening of 11 July 1912 as a high point of the 'Shakespeare's England' exhibition that had opened there in early May (*Times*, 10 May 1912, 11). The *Standard*'s report on 12 July, headed 'The Tourney at Earl's Court' (p. 11), was of course unsigned, but its comments on the mock-jousting performed by prominent members of the aristocracy and of London 'society' were sufficiently disenchanted (e.g., 'The mêlée with swords followed, nothing apparently happening except that the horses did not seem to be enjoying it very much') to warrant the possibility of their having indeed been written by Dugdale with TH's assistance.

45.2 *Monologue*: TH's reference is to the grandiose monument to the 3rd Earl of Bristol (d. 1698) and his two wives in the south transept of Sherborne Abbey, in Dorset. The Earl was survived by his second wife, and it is indeed her statue which occupies the position of privilege on his right hand and displays a memorial inscription distinctly warmer than that assigned to her predecessor on his left. For the texts of the inscriptions and other details, see Hutchins, iv. 253–4; for photographs, see *An Inventory of the Historical Monuments in the County of Dorset*, Volume I: *West Dorset* (London: Her Majesty's Stationery Office, 1952), plates 169, 170.

45.4 *We dug & dug*: unidentified, but conceivably related to the episode reported at *LW* 267.

45.6 *[Excision]*: nearly half of the leaf is cut away at the top; immediately following the excision are two essentially irrecoverable erased lines, suggesting that the excised text had perhaps been written over a pre-existing erasure.

45.8–9 *Another. . . . knew, &c*: a late addition squeezed in below the preceding line.

45.10 *D. Dialect*: TH had known William Barnes (see 7.5 n.) and admired his dialect verse (see, e.g., *Studies, Specimens*, 42–3, 43–4, 130–2, and *PV* 16–27, 291–7), but was himself determined to avoid categorization as a writer in dialect (see *PV* 11, 14, 28–9). He may nevertheless have hoped that thinking in dialect would give him greater access to the 'folk' origins of the ballad form.

45.11 *Incidents (of 1862–7, 1872, say)*: the years specified were especially important for TH. During the period 1862–7 he was for the first time living away from home, working in London as an architectural assistant, and trying to teach himself to be a poet, while 1872 was the year in which he abandoned architecture and decisively embarked on a career as a novelist. Shelley's 'A widow bird sate mourning for her Love', originally written as a song within the unfinished verse play *Charles the First*, was first published as 'A Song' in 1824 and later became especially well known because of its inclusion in *The Golden Treasury* of Francis Turner Palgrave. It consists of two quatrains, each with the first line iambic pentameter, the second and fourth iambic trimeter, and the third iambic tetrameter ($a^5b^3a^4b^3$ d.r.); cf. the common metre of hymnals ($a^4b^3a^4b^3$ d.r.), frequently used by TH. Shelley was always for TH 'the poet he loved' (*LW* 134) and 'the highest-soaring among all our lyricists' (*PV* 296); for other 'Poetical Matter' references to Shelley and his work, see 28.5, 39.9, 46.14, 49.10, 54.14, 65.7, 65.12–13, 79.6, and 81.8.

46.1   *The New View*: i.e., of the contrast between what, in 'Shut out that Moon', TH calls Life's 'Too fragrant . . . early bloom' and the 'Too tart . . . fruit it brought' (*CPW* i. 266). 'Shut out that Moon', dated 1904, was first published in *Time's Laughingstocks* in 1909. The quoted extracts from 'Memorial of the Unremembered', a poem of seven quatrains written by Edith M. Thomas and published in *The Century Magazine*, 69 (Feb. 1905), 533, are inscribed in ink in TH's hand on a pasted-in slip of paper, as is his identification of author and source.

46.9   *Songs of Things left to be divined*: cf. TH's note on '<u>Mystery Ballads</u>' at 63.12–13.

46.13–15   – *Also, after . . . unexplained.*: a late addition. TH's comment effectively captures the general character of the many short poems, categorized as 'Fragments', that Shelley deliberately left unfinished or undeveloped or that remained so as a consequence of his sudden and early death. For other references to Shelley, see 45.11 n.

46.16   *Poetry of the Microscope*: cf. 27.14, 39.2–4, and esp. 53.15–54.8, with its ideas on the 'Microscopic view of Nature', and *LW* 110. 'Also with Strength . . . manner?)' is a late addition. TH's interest in the work and influence of the German poet Heinrich Heine (1797–1856) long pre-dated the preparation and publication of his own first volume of verse, *Wessex Poems*, in 1898. He owned at least three editions of Heine's poems in translation (see 55.19 n.), visited Heine's grave when in Paris in 1890 (*LW* 240), and made a few translations of his own (evidently reworkings of existing translations) from Heine's collective *Buch der Lieder*, beginning with the first stanza of 'Lieb' Liebchen', from the 'Junge Leiden' ('Sorrows of Youth') section, in *Two on a Tower* (1882), ch. 11 (*W* 85); a second stanza, present in the serial, was omitted from the volume edition. Later came two lines of 'Götterdämmerung', from the 'Die Heimkehr' ('The Homecoming') section of *Buch der Lieder*, in *Jude the Obscure* (1896 [1895]), II. vi. (*W* 136), and the three stanzas of 'Ich stand in dunkeln Träumen', also from 'Die Heimkehr', published as 'Song from Heine' (*CPW* i. 223) in *Poems of the Past and the Present* (1902 [1901]). In this particular note TH seems to be referring not so much to the formal aspects of Heine's verse as to the frequent use of dialogue in many of his poems. For other references to Heine, see 49.11, 56.1, 61.11–12, and 62.1–2.

47.2   *The beauty in "Ugliness"*: cf. TH's note of 5 August 1888 at *LW* 222: 'To find beauty in ugliness is the province of the poet.' See also 58.1–9, *LW* 117–18, 123–4, and Bullen, 91–6. Although TH did not acknowledge George Crabbe (1754–1832; *OxfordDNB*) as a poetic influence, he certainly admired him as 'an apostle of realism' (*LW* 351) who had been important to him as a novelist. See also *PV* 225–6 and esp. *CL* v. 294. By English Art Club TH intends the New English Art Club, founded in 1886 by artists such as Sir George Clausen and Philip Wilson Steer, who had been influenced by French *plein-air* painting and were at odds with the conservatism of the Royal Academy. His note is clearly to be associated with the review of the Club's 1905 exhibition that he cut from *The Times* of 14 Oct. 1905 and inserted in 'Literary Notes II' (*LN* ii. 178–9).

47.7   *A calm day*: an almost identical note, supplemented by a parenthetical reference to Swanage, is at 5.2–3. The opening words of both lines of this note are written over essentially irrecoverable erasures.

47.10   *Lyrical Meth*: i.e., Lyrical Method. This note, inscribed in ink over erased pencil and originally marked with a now-erased '✕', is on a pasted-in cutting, possibly from a destroyed pocket-book. When read with its abbreviations expanded—'Find a situation from experience Turn to Lyrics for a form of expression that has been used for a quite different situation Use it (same situation from experience may be sung in several forms.)'—it can be recognized as a piece of advice that TH himself seems to have kept quite actively in mind: see Taylor, *Metres*, 73–4.

49.1   *As to rhyme*: Taylor (*Language*, 331) cites the first section of 'The Pine Planters' (*CPW* i. 328–9) as an instance of TH's occasionally increasing the density of the rhyme scheme in the concluding stanzas of his poems; for another example, see 'Shut out that Moon' (*CPW* i. 265–6, mentioned at 46.1–2). In *Winter Words* the quatrains of 'The Ballad of Love's Skeleton' (*CPW* iii. 269–71) rhyme *abcb* for eight stanzas and then change to *abab* for all but three of the remaining seven stanzas.

49.7   *Wordsworth in Ecclesiastical S.*: 'Confirmation', no. 23 of Part III of Wordsworth's 'Ecclesiastical Sonnets', was not in fact included in *The Poetical Works of William Wordsworth* (London: Routledge, Warne, & Routledge, 1864), the edition that TH owned and used in the 1860s (see *Studies, Specimens*, 91), but it was present (though unmarked) in his 8-vol. set of *The Poetical Works of William Wordsworth*, ed. William Knight (London: Macmilan, 1896), vii. 92. Both editions are in the DCM. 'Shelleyan view' apparently alludes to the frequent intrusion of intense melancholy into poems of Shelley's that are otherwise quite different in tone. For other references to Shelley, see 45.11 n.

49.11   *akin to Heine's*: Matthew Arnold's 'Heinrich Heine' essay (first published in 1863, collected in *Essays in Criticism: First Series* in 1865) seems to have been the principal source of TH's frequent identification of Heine as a leading exemplar of 'the modern spirit' (*LN* i. 106). *LN* reproduces and amply annotates the lengthy quotations from Arnold's essay that ELH transcribed into her husband's 'Literary Notes I' notebook (see *LN* i. 105–7, 345–6), probably in the mid-1870s: e.g., 'Heine's intense modernism, his absolute freedom, his utter rejection of stock classicism & stock romanticism[,] his bringing all things under the point of view of the nineteenth century . . .' (*LN* i. 106). Heine was also rousingly invoked by TH in the 1922 Apology to *Late Lyrics and Earlier*: 'Heine observed nearly a hundred years ago that the soul has her eternal rights; that she will not be darkened by statutes, nor lullabied by the music of bells' (*CPW* ii. 318). For TH's continuing interest in Heine and other 'Poetical Matter' references to him, see 46.16 n.

49.15   *we'll go no more a-roving*: the first quatrain of Byron's three-quatrain poem of 1817 reads: 'So, we'll go no more a-roving | So late into the night, | Though the heart be still as loving, | And the moon be still as bright.' Cf. TH's own poem 'Song to Aurore' (*CPW* iii. 224), beginning 'We'll not begin again to love', which was first collected in *Winter Words* following prior publication in the *Daily Telegraph* (Purdy,

261). For other 'Poetical Matter' references to Byron and his work, see 38.12, 54.14, 60.14, and 80.4 ff.

50.1 *"God" poems – continued from p . . . . :* see 40.16–41.4 and n.

50.2 *"To the Lesser God."*: several of the titles and phrases in this note recur in the similarly headed note at 72.1–5, where TH appears to be referring back, not to the present note, but to the note or 'still earlier notes' from which they both derived. 'about 1906': i.e., during the composition of *The Dynasts*. See also the note dated 5 February 1898 at *LW* 317.

50.12–14 *The mischievous . . . peace*: although the argument to which this passage is integral begins in Hartmann's *Philosophy of the Unconscious* (see 41.3 n.) at ii. 257, the specific quotation—slightly modified by TH, not least by his capitalization of 'will'—occurs at ii. 258: 'The consciousness here allowed, which has arisen only through the mischievous elevation of the quiescent will into volition, and must again cease with the return of the will to its original state of self-enclosed peace (all this will be proved and elucidated in Chap. xv. C.), can obviously give Theism no occasion to triumph at the necessity of a consciousness in the Unconscious.'

50.15 *Series of Ghostly poems*: 'P–'s' evidently refers to Poe, whose poems TH always admired (see *PV* 299–300 and *CL* ii. 303, v. 25); TH's copy of John H. Ingram's 4-vol. edition of *The Works of Edgar Allan Poe* (Edinburgh: Adam and Charles Black, 1874–5) is in the DCM. 'Marky' was one of ELH's cats, of a nervous disposition and consequently much persecuted by the other Max Gate cats: see, e.g., *CL* iii. 86, and *Letters of Emma and Florence Hardy*, ed. Michael Millgate (Oxford: Clarendon Press, 1996), 27. For 'God' as 'It', cf. 26.7–10 and n.

50.18 *It's better to suppose*: the reference is clearly to Blake's 'The Tyger': 'Did he who made the Lamb make thee?' The 'wherefore no one knows' phrase occurs within numerous poems (e.g., Alexander McLachlan's 'The rain it falls' of 1874).

51.2 *A new kind of poetry*: on the verso facing the page beginning with this note the microfilm of 'Poetical Matter' shows a narrow slip of paper, loosely inserted and apparently used as a bookmark, on which TH has written:

> The Greek Anthology ⊬ cloth
> "The Canterbury Poets"
>   Walter Scott, Warwick Lane

The note's format is suggestive of its having derived from an advertisement or review of *Selections from the Greek Anthology*, published in 'The Canterbury Poets' series (London: Walter Scott, [1889]). At the time of the book's first publication, however, TH had been given an inscribed copy (Beinecke) by its editor, the poet and miscellaneous writer Rosamund Tomson (later Rosamund Marriott Watson; *OxfordDNB*), to whom he was at the time sexually attracted. For TH's lingering memories of her, see 62.9–10; more generally, see *BR* 274–5 and especially Linda K. Hughes, *Graham R.: Rosamund Marriott Watson, Woman of Letters* (Athens: Ohio University Press, 2005), 91–3, etc.

The slip of paper itself has been torn off from what appears to have been a typed form letter, the verso of which TH had used for a verse draft: above the note already quoted are two erased verse lines, the second reading 'Promises that to-morrow shall be finer', perhaps an early version of what became l. 14 of 'An Unkindly May' (see 6.8 n.). Intruding into the first (irrecoverable) erased line are unerased descenders, possibly from a later draft of the same poem.

51.3 *Goya's "Desastres"*: the '1905 or 6' dating indicates that this note was originally written when TH was largely occupied with writing Part Second of *The Dynasts* (published February 1906) and therefore engaging extensively with the Spanish aspects of the Napoleonic wars. He would have known of *Los Desastres de la Guerra* by Francisco José de Goya y Lucientes, the famous series of etchings darkly reflective of those violent events—two examples were reproduced in William Rothenstein's *Goya* (London: at the Sign of the Unicorn, 1900), presented to him by Rothenstein at the time of its publication (*CL* ii. 266)—but access to the full series would perhaps have required a visit to the British Museum.

51.5 *Why should I care*: although identified as 'From old notes', these are evidently the notes themselves, written in ink, removed from their original context (presumably a pocket-book subsequently destroyed), pasted into 'Poetical Matter', and marked there with TH's shorthand symbol for 'poem' as potentially capable of development and completion. The concluding portion, beginning 'And for the love of telling', was originally inscribed on the verso of the slip that bears the title and concludes with an erased 'T.O.'; when TH was pasting the notes into 'Poetical Matter', however, he transcribed the three lines that were about to be obscured onto a second slip of paper that he then pasted to the bottom of the first. Additional writing on the verso is tantalizingly visible beneath 51.11–15 (see fig. 4) but only fragmentarily recoverable.

   The surviving draft verses constitute a rare and important example of TH's working methods as a poet. His warning to himself to avoid Swinburne's 'A Leave-taking'—included in that 1866 1st edition of *Poems and Ballads* to which he had responded so powerfully as a young man (see 17.6 n.)—was evidently prompted by the recognition that the 'Why should I care' structure with which he was working somewhat echoed the successive stanza openings of Swinburne's poem: e.g., 'Let us go hence, my songs; she will not hear' (stanza 1), 'Let us give up, go down; she will not care' (stanza 5), etc. For other 'Poetical Matter' references to Swinburne and his work, see 57.16, 58.1–9, 60.1, and 81.7.

53.10 *There might be*: the late additions to this note are '[address to a]' and the names following 'Unity S.' For TH's understanding of 'Faustina', see 17.6 n. 'Unity S.' was Unity Sargent, of Higher Bockhampton, one of the 'bevy now underground' (*LW* 233) whom TH remembered from his childhood and celebrated in the poem 'At Middle-field Gate in February' (*CPW* ii. 220–1). The identification of 'Mrs Tom D.' is somewhat problematic: Lieutenant Thomas Drane, R.N., the 'old navy lieutenant' mentioned in the opening paragraph of *LW*, seems not to have been married during his Higher Bockhampton retirement, and TH was perhaps referring to Drane's live-in mistress, whose story is invoked at 65.8, or to an altogether different 'Tom D.' 'Mrs P— O–den' was the wife (*née* Julia Henrietta Greathed) of William Parry Okeden, High Sheriff of Dorset at mid-century and owner of Turnworth House, in north Dorset, from 1846 until his death in 1868, when an extensive restoration of Turnworth church was funded in his memory. Turnworth House (demolished 1959) has long been identified as the original of Mrs Charmond's 'Hintock House' in *The Woodlanders*—notably by Bertram C. A. Windle, *The Wessex of Thomas Hardy* (London and New York: John Lane The Bodley Head, 1902), 169,

171—and since TH, overseeing the work on Turnworth church in 1869–70 (*BR* 106–7, 112), would have encountered Mrs Okeden early in her widowhood, it seems likely that his memories of her contributed something to his portrayal of the fictional Felice Charmond. Mrs Okeden is prominently mentioned in the report of the re-consecration of the church in the *Dorset County Chronicle*, 28 April 1870, 8, and although TH's own name does not appear, he was almost certainly present at the event and responsible for much if not all of the lengthy architectural description incorporated into the report (see *PV* 5–7). 'Lady Mary M—' has not been confidently identified.

53.15 *Charming set of Poems*: TH's interest in miniaturization, possibly owing something to Swift, has already emerged at 27.14, 39.2–4, and 46.16–47.1. The phrase 'or a brief statement in verse' is a late addition, as is the passage 'Also lichen . . . (about 1905)'. The likeliest source for 'Lady in the waterdrop' would appear to have been either Hans Christian Andersen's fairy-tale 'The Drop of Water' or the female figure detectable within a water bubble in the left foreground of Sir Joseph Noel Paton's 'fairy' painting 'The Reconciliation of Oberon and Titania', which TH could have seen when he visited Edinburgh in 1881 and 1909.

54.10 *Poems about the other side*: cf. TH's note, dated 17 July 1868, at *LW* 59: 'Perhaps I can do a volume of poems consisting of the *other side* of common emotions.'

54.13 *Simultaneousness*: it was in the early hours of 28 July 1814 that the 16-year-old Mary Godwin and Shelley (married and with two children) eloped from England to France in company with her step-sister Jane 'Claire' Clairmont; Mary Godwin married Shelley in 1816, following the suicide of his first wife, Harriet Westbrook. This complexly romantic story fascinated TH; see, e.g., *CL* ii. 169, iii. 86, 90, and *LW* 22, 44, 327. For other 'Poetical Matter' references to Shelley, see 45.11 n. 'H.' is Hampstead.

54.16 *People at Agricultural Show*: the Dorchester Agricultural Show was an annual event of local importance, and since the two preceding notes are dated 1906, TH may possibly have visited the 65th show, held on 28 September 1906 (*Dorset County Chronicle*, 4 Oct. 1906, 5–6).

55.3 *The Ford. (Ballad)*: '[Meth Heads only].' (where 'Meth' is again an abbreviation of 'Method') has been retrospectively added above the line and marked with a double rule for emphasis; it appears to specify that, given the intended ballad mode, only the principal elements of the story would be narrated within the poem. 'Anketell' is an earlier (though not extinct) and more metrically convenient spelling of 'Antell', the family with which TH was connected through the marriage of his aunt, Mary Hand, to the Puddletown shoemaker John Antell in 1847; see 28.5 n. and 57.15 n. See also Hutchins, iv. 513, for an Anketill [*sic*] pedigree dated 1623. 'B.ʳ' is brother and 'f.ʳ' is father.

55.19 *[Told . . . "Marie H . . ."*: inscribed over an erased, square-bracketed, and apparently substantively similar note; TH's erasure and reinscription provided him with sufficient space to add the note's final two sentences. 'Marie H . . .' is the ballad 'Marie Hamilton' or 'The Queen's Marie'; cf. 43.5–7 and 70.1–5, where reference is made to its 'Sudden leaps of thought'. 'Tod.ᵉʳ' refers to John Todhunter's translation of the 3rd edition of *Buch der Lieder* as *Heine's Book of Songs* (Oxford: at the Clarendon Press, 1907). Also in TH's library were the heavily marked *Heine's Book of Songs*, trans. Charles G. Leland (New York: Henry Holt and Company, 1881), and the more lightly marked *The Poems of Heine Complete*, trans. Edgar Alfred Bowring (London: George Bell and Sons, 1878), but Todhunter's volume is the one specifically invoked in 'Poetical Matter' (cf. 61.11–12). For other 'Poetical Matter' references to Heine, see 46.16 n. The same basic ballad plot that is here headed 'The Ford' does indeed appear in 'The Brother' (*CPW* iii. 218), subsequently published in *Winter Words* (cf. 72.12 n.).

56.3   *Crossing Ewelease*: for the ewelease itself, see 30.12 n.; 'B.' is [Higher] Bockhampton. The 'something of this kind in verse' half-remembered by TH was presumably 'Night in the Old Home' (*CPW* i. 325–6), first published in *Time's Laughingstocks* in 1909.

56.7   *Rejected from "The Dynasts*: for other ideas not drawn upon in *The Dynasts*, see the entries that TH copied into his 'Memoranda II' notebook in 1922 (*PN* 58–9) and that FEH subsequently included in the penultimate chapter of *The Later Years of Thomas Hardy*, published over her own name in 1930 (see *LW* 449–50).

57.6   *The Bitter in the Sweet*: for '"Our sweet enemy" (France)', cf. 'that sweet enemy, France' (Sidney, *Astrophel and Stella*, sonnet 41). 'There's a'ways something' is a proverbial assertion (possibly derived from TH's mother) of the fundamental contradictoriness of the world. 'my hated Love' is probably TH's adaptation of Catullus's 'odi et amo' (*Carmina*, no. 85), though 'my hated Love' does appear in Richard Fanshawe's translation of Battista Guarini's *Il Pastor Fido* (*The Faithful Shepherd*), I. iii. 124, and 'Thou hated Love' occurs in Phineas Fletcher's 'A Vow'. The remaining oxymorons appear to be TH's own inventions.

57.11   *Subdramatic*: James Fotheringham, in *Studies in the Poetry of Robert Browning* (London: Kegan Paul, Trench & Co., 1887), defines *Paracelsus* as 'subdramatic poetry', but argues that poems of Browning's conventionally characterized as '"*dramatic thinking*" or "*dramatic apology*," as if the primary and final interest were intellectual', do in fact possess a 'true dramatic quality', involving 'the person, not the mind only' (pp. 54, 57–8). The passage quoted by TH continues: 'and a voice like the voice of life, though the work all the same is intellectual, not vital; abstract, not concrete' (p. 58).

57.14   *in style of thought*: the meaning of the shorthand is unclear, but the crudely formed characters are perhaps intended to represent 'paradox' (a concept TH explores in the immediately following entries).

57.15   *The man who had no friend*: TH's uncle by marriage John Antell senior, the radical Puddletown shoemaker (see 28.5 n.), was very much of his time and class in responding with anger, alcohol, and violence to the social deprivations and intellectual frustrations that were his daily experience. His last years were made yet more difficult and painful by the onset of a wasting disease that was almost certainly cancer. See *BR* 100, 319–20, and the self-posed photograph following p. 116. Added later to the note was the link to 'Two Leaders', from Swinburne's *Poems and Ballads. Second Series* (1878), with its paradoxical response to John Henry Newman and Thomas Carlyle and its key line, 'With all our hearts we praise you whom ye hate' (see *LW* 372), that TH evidently found expressive of his own feelings towards Antell. For other references to Swinburne, see 51.5 n.

58.1   *The beautiful in the commonplace*: TH's quotation, accurate in all essentials (apart from the inserted exclamation mark within square brackets), is taken from p. 6 of the unsigned obituary of Swinburne in the *Academy* (17 Apr. 1909), 5–7. For

TH's admiration of Swinburne, see 17.6 n. and 51.5 n.; for another note—and TH's views—on the beautiful in the commonplace, see 47.2–6 and n.

58.12–14   *The virtuous Emp. . . . Tyana*: TH's essentially accurate quotation is from the review of T. R. Glover's *The Conflict of Religions in the Early Roman Empire* (London: Methuen & Co., 1909) published in *The Times Literary Supplement*, 24 June 1909, 229–30. To the anonymous reviewer the multiple images from different religions suggested that if Christianity had been less radical 'it would have enjoyed the same toleration as the rest'. Though TH recorded all details of the book, including its price, there seems to have been no copy in the Max Gate library. 'Severus' was Marcus Aurelius Severus Alexander, Emperor 222–35 CE, said to have been virtuous but vacillating and ineffective. A lararium was the part of a Roman house devoted to the 'lares' (household deities). Apollonius of Tyana, neo-Pythagorean philosopher and teacher (*c*.3–*c*.97 CE), appears to have been venerated as a worker of miracles both before and after his death.

58.17   *After the Monmouth rising*: the armed rising of 1685 in support of the Protestant Duke of Monmouth against the Catholic King James II was largely confined to the west of England, and when it collapsed following Monmouth's defeat at the Battle of Sedgemoor, in Somerset, on 6 July 1685, some of the scattered survivors of the battle fled into Dorset—as in TH's short story 'The Duke's Reappearance'. Monmouth himself was quickly captured and executed, and many of his supporters subsequently received savage punishments, including death and transportation, at the hands of Judge Jeffreys during the so-called 'Bloody Assize' held in Dorchester itself, the county town. TH seems to have believed that one of his mother's relatives of an earlier generation had been among those transported (*LW* 10–11), but the anecdote here appears to have been invented or perhaps adapted from elsewhere. 'Rizpah' refers to Tennyson's poem, first published in 1880 in *Ballads and Other Poems*; see also 2 Sam. 21: 8–10.

59.8–10   *And thanked God . . . men are*: an obvious echo of the Pharisee's words in the parable of the Pharisee and the publican; see Luke 18: 10–14.

59.14   *The Unborn & the Dead*: for a lively and relevant prose precedent of which TH was almost certainly unaware, see James Henry, 'Dialogue between a Stethoscopist and an Unborn Child', appended with separate pagination (pp. 1–14) to his *A Half Year's Poems* (Dresden: Printed by C. C. Meinhold and Sons, 1854), and reprinted in *Selected Poems of James Henry*, ed. Christopher Ricks (New York: Other Press, 2002), 66–77.

59.16   *A man has written*: Swinburne's first collection of *Poems and Ballads* (see 17.6 n.), strongly attacked for its sexual and other improprieties at the time of its first appearance in 1866, was subsequently judged to have contained his best work. For other references to Swinburne, see 51.5 n.

60.4–5   *Speak of everyday . . . across them*: the quotation, from the anarchistic writings of Zo d'Axa (1864–1930), born Alphonse Gallaud de la Pérouse, appeared in the *Quarterly Review*, 179 (Oct. 1894), 295, within the context of 'The Strike of a Sex', a strident attack—published anonymously but written by the Catholic apologist William Francis Barry (1849–1930), a frequent reviewer for the *Quarterly*—on the contemporary phenomenon of the New Woman as described or represented in several recent works of fiction and sociology. The immediate occasion of the quotation was Sarah Grand's *The Heavenly Twins* (1893), just previously described as not so much 'original' as 'aboriginal', but while TH had referred somewhat dismissively to that same novel in a letter to Florence Henniker (*CL* ii. 18), his concern here is clearly with the wider implications of the quotation itself, which read in full: 'It is simple enough. If our extraordinary flights (*nos fugues inattendues*) throw people out a little, the reason is that we speak of everyday things as the primitive barbarian would, were he brought across them.' '[good for poetry . . . prose.]' is a late addition.

60.7–8 *Who seems . . . alone*: line 195 of George Puttenham's *Partheniades*, a sequence of poems in praise of Queen Elizabeth, apparently dating from 1579, that was reprinted on a number of occasions during the nineteenth century. TH probably encountered it in *Ballads from Manuscripts*, vol. 2, 'Part II. Ballads Relating Chiefly to the Reign of Queen Elizabeth', ed. W. R. Morfill (Hertford: Printed for The Ballad Society by Stephen Austin and Sons, 1873), 79:

> Affable grace, speeche eloquent and wise,
> Stately præsence, suche as becometh one
> Whoe seemes to rule realmes by her lookes alone.

The inversion noted by TH consists in the substitution of a trochee for an iamb for the third foot ('realmes by') of what is otherwise regular iambic pentameter.

60.13–14 *(metre. Farewell . . . prayer.)*: a late addition. The reference is to Byron's 'Farewell! if ever fondest prayer' with its two iambic tetrameter octaves ($a^4b^4a^4b^4c^4b^4c^4$ $b^4d^4b^4d^4d^4c^4d^4c^4$ d.r.). TH used the metre and rhyme scheme of the first stanza in several poems; see Taylor, *Metres*, 247. For other 'Poetical Matter' references to Byron, see 49.15 n.

60.15–61.1 *A painting . . . power*: TH's source, an anonymous review of C. J. Holmes's *Notes on the Art of Rembrandt* in *The Times Literary Supplement*, 7 Dec. 1911, reads: 'It is not wonderful that [Rembrandt] should have made so many etchings and drawings, for in these he had more mastery over matter than was possible in paint. A drawing or an etching can make no pretence of a complete representation of reality. Line is a convention in its very nature and, because of its limited powers of representation, has a greater power of expression' (p. 497). Although by condensing this passage (more fully and accurately transcribed at *LN* ii. 208) TH somewhat misrepresented it, his having nevertheless extracted from it a perception germane to his own poetic purposes is indicated by his illustrative quotation of the opening lines of a children's game found in many parts of the British Isles: see, e.g., Iona and Peter Opie, *The Singing Game* (Oxford: Oxford University Press, 1985), 239–42. Most recorded versions of the game begin with 'Green gravel', but the earlier and more expressive 'Green grave O' seems to have survived somewhat longer in Dorset: see the Revd Herbert Pentin, 'Dorset Children's Doggerel Rhymes', *Proceedings of the Dorset Natural History and Antiquarian Field Club*, 38 (1918), [112]–32. Cf. *CL* v. 279.

61.8 *Dreamery*: evidently invoked by TH in the second of the two senses recognized in the *OED*: 'Dream-work, "such stuff as dreams are made of [*sic*]"'. Cf. the opening lines of 'A Wife Comes Back' (*CPW* ii. 368). TH would in any case have been keenly aware of the translations from Heine included under the heading 'Dream Pictures' in the early pages of Todhunter's volume: see next annotation.

61.11–12   *H—e 124 Tod.*: TH's reference to p. 124 of John Todhunter's *Heine's Book of Songs* (see 55.19 n.) is not entirely clear: three poems appear or begin on p. 124 itself, and almost all of the poems at this point in the volume treat of death and graves. Beginning on the facing p. 125, however, is 'Night lay upon my eyelids', Todhunter's translation of 'Nacht lag auf meinen Augen', from the *Lyrisches Intermezzo* ('Lyrical Intermezzo') sequence, spoken specifically from within a grave.

61.3   *Having left something behind*: cf. 18.15–16.

62.1–2   *H—e metre*: TH is presumably referring to the frequent use of seven-syllable lines (usually iambic tetrameter catalectic) in Heine's songs as translated by Todhunter; see, e.g., nos. LXII and LXIV of 'Lyrical Intermezzo' on pp. 124 and 125–7 (see 61.11–12 n.), where most of the first and third lines are catalectic in otherwise largely regular ballad stanzas ($a^4b^3c^4b^3$ d.r.). 'Another . . . "Nelson".' is a late addition. 'The Duel' (*CPW* ii. 184–5), set in the reign of Charles II and based on a note in TH's 'Facts' notebook (*Facts*, 317–18), was first published in *Moments of Vision* in 1917. Sir William Hamilton (1731–1803) was the wealthy diplomat and art collector whose second wife, Emma Hamilton, formerly his mistress, later became the mistress of Horatio Nelson, the famous British admiral. Their resulting *ménage à trois* (referred to in the *Dictionary of National Biography*) ended in 1803 when Hamilton died in London in the presence of both Emma and Nelson after having in his will left the former a substantial annual allowance and the latter a portrait of Emma.

62.5   *A woman Ariel*: in Shakespeare's *The Tempest*, v. i. 93–4, the couplet concluding Ariel's 'Where the bee sucks' song reads: 'Merrily, merrily shall I live now | Under the blossom that hangs on the bough'. The suggestion of 'lie' as an alternative to 'live' was presumably intrinsic to TH's thought rather than an indication of doubt as to the Shakespearian text.

62.7   *Theocritus*: TH invokes the third-century BCE Greek pastoral poet Theocritus in commemoration of the traditional aspects of life in the isolated rural hamlet of Higher Bockhampton where he had lived throughout his childhood; see *BR* 38. TH's copy of *Theocritus, Bion and Moschus*, trans. Andrew Lang (London: Macmillan, 1889), is at the Harry Ransom Center, University of Texas at Austin; cf. *LW* 212.

62.9   *A letter comes*: for Graham Tomson, see 51.2 n. 'He fears to open it.' and '(delayed in P. O. say)' are late additions, perhaps inserted on separate occasions.

62.12   *Ancient Greek poem*: TH does not suggest why or when such a poem might be 'required'; his imagination of St Paul's reception at Ephesus by the worshippers of Diana of the Ephesians is based on Acts 19. '(children?)' is a late addition.

63.2   *Cerne Union*: the 'Union' or workhouse just outside Cerne Abbas (see 37.6 n.) was built in 1836 but closed and sold off in 1929; the building still stands and is currently a residential home for the elderly. Just across the valley, cut into the turf on the facing hillside and outlined in chalk, is the huge prehistoric and emphatically phallic figure known as the Cerne Giant: see John Newman and Nikolaus Pevsner, *The Buildings of England: Dorset* (Harmondsworth: Penguin Books, 1972), 135 and illustration 6.

63.3 *Lady elopes with groom*: this 'old note' is directly related to, and probably preceded in point of original composition, the extended anecdote that TH subsequently inserted in its entirety (adding a prefatory note headed 'The Lady who declined') into 'Poetical Matter' at 74.7–75.9. 'Evangeline', Henry Wadsworth Longfellow's long narrative poem, written in unrhymed hexameters, would have been familiar to TH ever since he had been given a copy of Longfellow's *Poetical Works* (Beinecke) in 1859. 'Style St. & B.', repeated at 74.1, is apparently an abbreviation for 'Style[:] Statement and Ballad', where the 'Statement' (cf. 54.1) is the initial indication of narrative context prior to the beginning of the ballad proper. See 65.8 n. for the example of 'Keith of Ravelston', which TH may already have had in mind.

63.10 "*Mindsights*": see 3.10 and n.; for Balaam and the angel of the Lord, see Num. 22: 20–35.

63.12 *Mystery Ballads*: cf. 46.9–15.

64.6 *Content with injustice*: a brief emergence of TH's sympathy for animals, although he curiously omits from his selective quotation the line in the first stanza of Henry Vaughan's 'The Bird' in which the injustice of nature is particularly signalled: 'Many a sullen storm, | For which coarse man seems much the fitter born, | Rain'd on thy bed | And harmless head' (ll. 3–6). The spelling 'coarse' in the omitted sentence is that of TH's copy (DCM) of Vaughan's *Sacred Poems and Pious Ejaculations*, ed. H. F. Lyte (London: George Bell and Sons, 1897), and of other nineteenth-century editions, while twentieth-century editions generally prefer 'course.' Cf. *CL* v. 194.

64.9 *Poem by a Being*: cf. 65.2–7.

64.15–65.1 *The whole incomprehensible . . . Allies*: quoted from one of Aldous Huxley's frequent 'Marginalia' contributions (signed 'Autolycus') as first published in the *Athenæum*, 20 Aug. 1920, 243. Prompted by the sounds of dripping water, it was later revised and included as 'Water Music' in Huxley's *On the Margin* (London: Chatto & Windus, 1923). As of 1920 the Allied Powers of the First World War were still differing over the implementation of various decisions arrived at during the Versailles Conference of 1919.

65.2 *A timeless poem*: cf. 64.9–14 and the reflections on time in TH's 'The Absolute Explains', first published in February 1925, and 'So, Time', both collected in *Human Shows* (*CPW* iii. 68–72). The scene from *A Pair of Blue Eyes*, ch. 22 (*W* 242), was earlier invoked at 38.9–11. 'Ozymandias' is Shelley's famous poem of that title; it seems now to be accepted that Ozymandias was a Hellenized form of the prenomen of the pharaoh Ramesses II and that the ruins, now known as the Ozymandias Colossus, were those of Ramesses' mortuary temple. *La Légende des Siècles* was conceived, though never fully realized, by Victor Hugo as an extended series of poems chronicling the progress through time of Man himself, 'cette grande figure une et multiple, lugubre et rayonnante, fatale et sacrée, l'Homme' (Préface de Victor Hugo, *La Légende des Siècles*, ed. Paul Berret (Paris: Librairie Hachette, 1920), i. 12). Cf. *LN* i. 170 and ii. 459–60. For TH on Hugo, see *LW* 334, *CL* iii. 81, and *TH Remembered*, 285.

65.8 *Ballad*: 'in manner previously noted' evidently refers back to 'Style St. & B.' at 63.8 (see n.); TH's supplementary 'mem.' (memorandum) refers to the ballad-within-poem structure exemplified by 'Keith of Ravelston', the untitled narrative sequence in ballad form that constitutes the greater part of the poem 'A Nuptial Eve' by Sydney Dobell (1824–74) in *The Poems of Sydney Dobell* (London: Walter Scott, 1887), 136–8. TH's copy is in the Harry Ransom Center, University of Texas at Austin. 'T. Cox' is identified by Brenda Tunks, in *Whatever Happened to the Other Hardys?* (Poole: Brenda Tunks, 1990), 75–6, as Thomas Cox, the son of John Cox, the local Registrar for Births and Deaths, who lived in Higher Bockhampton in what TH called 'The House of Hospitalities' (*CPW* i. 255). TH had evidently heard much local gossip about Thomas Cox's having in 1842 married Jemima Paul, a servant in the nearby household of former naval lieutenant Thomas Drane, even though she was eight years older than Cox and already had an illegitimate 5-year-old son. See the entry in the 'Memoranda I' notebook (*PN* 28–9)—dated November 1901 and specified as material for a short story—where it is said that Paul (there incorrectly spelled Pawle) had been Drane's mistress and that Cox was bribed to marry her. In light of the reference to 'Mrs Tom D.' at 53.11, it seems possible that Jemima Paul had at one point called herself, or been regarded as, Drane's wife. William R. O'Byrne's *A Naval Biographical Dictionary* (London: John Murray, 1849) identifies 1842 as the year in which Drane was accepted as an out-pensioner of the naval hospital at Greenwich.

65.10 *Chorus of any future drama*: apparently one that might be written by TH himself. Helen is Helen of Troy; for Potiphar's wife, see Gen. 39: 7–20; for Bathsheba, see 2 Sam. 11: 1–27; for Jael, see Judg. 4: 17–22 and 5: 24–7; for Faustina, see above 17.6 n.; for Mary Magdalene, see Matt. 27: 55–61, Mark 15: 40–7, 16: 1–9, etc. TH invoked Helen, Bathsheba, Jael, and Cleopatra in 'The Clasped Skeletons' (*CPW* iii. 209–11), first collected in *Winter Words*, following prior publication in the *Daily Telegraph* (Purdy, 261).

65.12–13 *And like a dying lady*: the opening words of Shelley's posthumously-published six-line fragment 'The Waning Moon'. The complete first line reads: 'And like a dying lady, lean and pale'.

66.2 *"K. of Rav^u"*: see 65.8–9 and n.

66.3 *Xmas party at Lesnewth*: during his lengthy courtship of Emma Gifford TH made a number of visits to the isolated Cornish parish of St Juliot, where she was living at the rectory with her sister and her sister's husband, the Revd Caddell Holder, and it was probably in late December 1872 that he accompanied them to this party in the neighbouring parish of Lesnewth. The 'locket' was presumably the one containing Emma's portrait that is now in the Berg collection at the New York Public Library, and TH's sensitivity to its 'clink' was perhaps related to the presence of the Lesnewth churchwarden whom he believed to have been a rival for Emma's affections. See *BR* 119 and 'The Young Churchwarden' (*CPW* ii. 193–4). TH's 'Burning the Holly' (*CPW* iii. 228–31), first collected in *Winter Words* following prior publication in the *Daily Telegraph* (Purdy, 261), was evidently in existence by the time this note was written.

66.12 *Rain has been*: for 'ewelease stile', see 30.12 n. 'F. Moor' is Fordington Moor, the low-lying area of marshland and meadow, just east of Dorchester, to which TH gave the fictional name of Durnover Moor. Cf. 3.19 and see *The Mayor of Casterbridge*, ch. 40 (*W* 328), and Hermann Lea, *Thomas Hardy's Wessex* (London: Macmillan, 1913), 104.

67.1   *Woodyates Inn*: this draft, evidently derived from 'The Aged Bagman' (69.2–71.11), is roughly written in pencil on the versos of leaves from two different typed circulars that have been clipped or pinned together at the top left corner, inserted (apparently quite loosely) in 'Poetical Matter', and photographed across a two-page opening. The first circular solicits funds for Toc H, the church-based social-activist movement founded during the First World War by the Revd Philip Thomas Byard ('Tubby') Clayton (1885–1972); the second, from a broker offering his services in the purchase of shares, incorporates a reply form that is conveniently pre-dated 'November, 1927', a clear indication that TH inscribed the draft shortly before he finally stopped working in his study. The second page of the draft begins at 68.10, where TH has added 'Woodyates' to indicate that the following stanzas are a continuation. TH's marking of the draft's first line suggests that he was considering several possible readings: 'From first to last much have [has] been seen', 'Of first to last much . . .', 'Of first and last much . . .', 'Much have [has] been seen first and last', etc. In the second line the horizontal rule following 'Aye!' allows for the repetition of whichever reading has been selected in the first line. The deletions of word and line fragments throughout (indicated in the edited text) and the words inscribed over dashes at 67.13, 67.16, and 68.14 (not indicated in the edited text) give some sense of how TH hastily revised the draft while in the process of writing it.

Woodyates Inn was an old coaching-inn (no longer in existence) on the London road between Salisbury and Blandford. For TH's interest in the inn, especially as a stopping place for George III and members of his family when travelling between London and Weymouth, see *LW* 421–2, *Facts*, 8–9, and *PN* 131. A 'bagman' was not, as in North American usage, a collector or distributor of illicit funds, but rather 'A commercial traveller, whose business it is to show samples and solicit orders on behalf of manufacturers, etc.' (*OED*). At 68.18 'elewise' is TH's slip for 'elsewise'.

69.2   *The Aged Bagman*: the prose narrative that evidently provided the starting point both for the accompanying draft stanzas and for 'Woodyates Inn' has been written on the verso of a typed form letter advertising the New York *Forum* magazine and dated 29 May 1923. However, the title itself, the three stanzas immediately below it (written in two columns separated by a vertical rule, the second column beginning 'I was a thriving bagman'), and the notes on the present tense and 'Marie Hamilton' seem to have been written on a separate slip of paper that was then superimposed upon, hence obscuring, roughly the top third of the prose narrative. The resulting item has been folded upward and attached at its head to the notebook's inside gutter. Most of the numerous corrections and insertions affecting both the verse and the prose texts were apparently made during the initial inscription process, with two clear exceptions: 'having been a gentleman of the road at an earlier day' (70.6–7) was added to the slip of paper containing the stanzas after it had been fixed in place, and the concluding stanza (71.6–11) is squeezed in at the foot of the verso of the typed letter following the conclusion of the prose narrative. This stanza is written in two columns: the first consists of the two opening lines written over three erased lines (variants of what are now the second and third lines), and the second, beginning 'And when white with grief', is arrowed in for insertion after the first.

For TH's query as to the poem's continuing in the present tense, cf. 71.14–17. TH's note on the 'Sudden leaps of thought' in 'Marie H$^{\underline{n}}$' (the ballad 'Marie

Hamilton') is a word-for-word repetition of 43.5–7; see also 55.19. A 'gentleman of the road' is a highwayman.

71.15–17 *It dispenses . . . prophet*: selectively quoted from 'Studies in Literary Psychology. III. Carlyle and the Present Tense', an article by Vernon Lee (the pseudonym of Violet Paget, 1856–1935; *OxfordDNB*) first published in the *Contemporary Review*, 85 (Mar. 1904), 386–92, but presumably quoted here from her *The Handling of Words and Other Studies in Literary Psychology* (London: John Lane The Bodley Head, 1923), 181–2. TH knew Vernon Lee at least to the extent of calling on her and her half-brother Eugene Lee-Hamilton when visiting Florence with ELH in 1887, and he would certainly have been aware of her negative comments on his own writing style, first published in the *English Review* of September 1911, that were also included in *The Handling of Words*. Although TH's quotation specifically invokes Thomas Carlyle, it seems clear from his heading that he was chiefly interested in Vernon Lee's advocacy of the present tense itself: e.g., '*the present tense makes things present*; it abolishes the narrative and the narrator' (p. 175; Lee's italics).

72.1 *Paean to the Lesser God*: copied from an 'old note' already revisited at greater length at 50.2–9.

72.7 "*Two Trees*": cf. 13.11–17 and n. 'might please' is written over an irrecoverable erasure.

72.12 <u>*Good tragic ballad*</u>: the copying of this early note into 'Poetical Matter' at so late a point seems to indicate that TH had not yet destroyed all of his working pocket-books. Outlined at 55.3–18 is another tragic ballad involving the murder of a secretly married man by his wife's sibling, followed by TH's recollection of his having already written the similarly plotted 'The Brother', subsequently included in *Winter Words* (cf. 55.19 n.).

72.15 *A suffering God*: see 25.1–4 for this same note, identically dated and almost identically phrased; cf. also 40.16–41.4 and 50.10–11.

73.3 <u>*Moods towards Nature*</u>: a rare example of TH's initial poetic development of an idea originating in a note, specifically the note on 'the pathos of nature' at 40.17–18. At 73.9 TH wrote and then erased a line of dashes and '[Nothing disturbs her equanimity]', but subsequently reinscribed the comment and expanded upon it.

74.1 <u>*The Lady who declined*</u>: TH's development of the narrative idea summarized in the 'Lady elopes with groom' note at 63.3–8. 'Style S. & B.' refers back to the pattern of 'statement' followed by 'ballad' invoked in that note and exemplified by Sydney Dobell's 'A Nuptial Eve' (see 65.8 n.), although the draft stanzas here are tetrameter triplets rather than the rhymed hexameters earlier proposed. The present entry is composed of three distinct elements: (1) the '<u>Prefatory note</u>' inscribed directly in pencil on the recto of a 'Poetical Matter' leaf; (2) the prose narrative inscribed in ink on a leaf of smaller unruled paper that has itself been cut laterally in two (following 'rudiments' at 75.3), the first segment being inserted in 'Poetical Matter' immediately following the Prefatory note and the second pasted to the verso of the same leaf; (3) pasted to the same verso, the two draft triplets marked '<u>Begin</u>', written in ink on the back of a slip from a typed promotional circular for a 'deservedly popular security' ('Next dividend due 1st July').

For TH's lifelong fascination with and the autobiographical significance of 'Poor Man and the Lady' plots, see *BR* 50, 103, and Patricia Ingham, *Thomas Hardy* (Hemel Hempstead: Harvester Wheatsheaf, 1989), 45–55. The suggestion that the groom's father 'may be carpenter or mason' is also significant in view of TH's own father's trade of mason (see *BR* 29–30). For 'the strains of a violin', cf. the seduction by violin in TH's story 'The Fiddler of the Reels'. 'Delalynde', or De la Lynde, was an ancient Dorset family name well known to TH because of the local legend of a thirteenth-century De la Lynde's killing a beautiful deer that King Henry III had spared when hunting: see *Tess*, ch. 2 (*W* 10). However, neither a Rosa nor a Sir Hugh De la Lynde is included in the family pedigree given in Hutchins, iv. 479.

76.1   *? [1863–7]*: this entry—the earliest dated entry in 'Poetical Matter'—is inscribed, almost entirely in ink, on two leaves of faintly ruled paper evidently excised from one of TH's destroyed pocket-books. The first leaf, comprised of a recto page numbered in pencil 161 and a perhaps unnumbered verso, is hinged to the 'Poetical Matter' page by a strip of paper pasted along the verso's right-hand edge, resulting in some minor obliterations of the verso's text, possibly including the number 162. The editors have supplied obscured word-endings and punctuation without introducing square brackets into the edited text at 76.17 ('fam[ily.]'), 76.19 ('discove[ry]'), 78.6 ('oppos[ed]'), 78.8 ('come[s –]'), 78.9 ('kis[ses]'), and 78.10 ('do[or.]'). The second leaf, beginning 'They see the priest' (78.12), has been pasted down—obliterating its verso—alongside the first leaf on the same 'Poetical Matter' page, so that when the first's recto (161) is turned over to the left—across the concluding elements of 'The Lady who declined'—the first's verso ([162]) and the second's recto (163, numbered in ink) are open side by side. Small tears in the top left corners of the two detached leaves suggest that they were at one point clipped together before being separated for insertion in 'Poetical Matter'.

The date '? [1863–7]' appears to be a late addition. TH's thus assigning the poem outline only very generally to the period he had spent in London as an architectural assistant with poetic aspirations is strongly suggestive of his having attempted to date the leaves well after detaching them from their original location. 'July 18.' is also a late addition, although clearly inserted earlier than '? [1863–7]'. '[good]', the alternative readings 'sitting' and 'leaning', and '[Rhyme only 2nd & 4$^{\underline{th}}$ lines]' were all evidently added, in pencil, at or after the entry's insertion in 'Poetical Matter', whereas '[This ballad was never finished]', written over a largely irrecoverable ink erasure concluding 'façade', was clearly of earlier date and perhaps contemporary with the original inscription. The draft verses are indeed written in 'ballad metre' ($a^4b^3c^4b^3$ d.r.) and therefore 'Rhyme only 2nd & 4$^{\underline{th}}$ lines'.

The prose narrative originally began in the third person, switching to the first person with 'I tell my tale' (76.15–16). TH subsequently changed all the prose instances of first person to third person, sometimes by writing over the original pronouns and altering the verb forms (not indicated in the edited text) and sometimes by strike-throughs and interlineations (indicated in the edited text). Thus TH altered 'I tell my tale' to 'He tells his tale' by writing 'He' over 'I', adding an 's' to 'tell', striking through 'my', and inserting 'his' above the line (see fig. 5). At 76.16 'He' is the landlord, as was of course clear when the narrative was told in the first person. At 78.13 'ivory,' is a late addition. 'That a curse is upon her – ' was retrospectively inserted above the line, replacing the erased but still visible 'End' which immediately preceded 'she is <u>dumb</u>' (cf. Tennyson's 'The Lady of Shalott': '"The curse is come upon me", cried | The Lady of Shalott'). To the right of 'Six times replièd she:' at 79.2 is an erased reiteration of the same phrase.

79.6   *Shades of the Lyrists*: this heading is written over a largely irrecoverable erasure, apparently a single-line description of the idea behind this detailed scenario, perhaps imagined as something for eventual stage or radio presentation by the 'Hardy Players' or some other local group; see Keith Wilson, *Thomas Hardy on Stage* (Basingstoke: Macmillan, 1995). TH, who would have encountered 'Lyrists', a rarely used term for 'lyric poet', in Shelley's *Adonais*, stanza xxx ('The sweetest lyrist of her saddest wrong'), elsewhere referred to Shelley himself as 'our most marvellous lyrist' (*LW* 22). It is perhaps relevant that the reference in *Adonais* was to Thomas Moore and that Shelley had invoked Byron (see next two annotations) earlier in the same stanza.

79.8   *"When he who adores thee"*: a song written by Thomas Moore (1779–1852; *OxfordDNB*) to an old air 'The Fox Sleeps'. Moore was buried in Bromham churchyard in 1852, having spent his last years at Sloperton Cottage, near Calne, Wiltshire, and close to Bowood, the seat of Lord Lansdowne, at this stage his strongest supporter and patron. 'or voice of Moore afar.' and '(handsome young witches?)' are late additions.

80.4   *"When we two parted."*: poem by Byron, who died in Greece in April 1824; his body was returned (against his wishes) to England, and buried in the family vault in Hucknall Torkard churchyard near the Byrons' ancestral home of Newstead Abbey, Nottinghamshire. For other references to Byron, see 49.15 n. 'or voice of B. afar.' is a late addition.

80.14   *"O Brignall Banks"*: by Scott, originally published in Canto III of *Rokeby*, and subsequently much reprinted as a separate poem. Dryburgh Abbey aisle is the location of Scott's tomb, one of several places associated with Scott that TH visited while staying in southern Scotland with his friend Sir George Douglas in September 1891. See *LW* 250–1 and *TH Remembered*, 64. 'on N. wind' is a late addition; 'snag' is defined by the *OED* as 'sloe' (i.e., sloe gin).

81.11–12   *Mocking Bird (Christy)*: the song 'Listen to the Mockingbird', rather surprisingly included here, was first published in 1855 and became famous on both sides of the Atlantic. It was, however, composed and written by Septimus Winner (using the pseudonym Alice Hawthorne), and not by Edwin P. Christy (1815–62), the American originator of Christy's Minstrels, the well-known 'minstrel show', for which 'Listen to the Mockingbird' was a perennial standard, regularly included in successive editions of *The Christy's Minstrels' Song Book*. Christy had in fact retired in 1854, before 'Mockingbird' was published, but the group continued under the leadership of George N. Harrington (who assumed the name Christy), and TH very probably saw one or more of its London performances. That he thought 'Mockingbird' a charming song is evident from its invocation in 'The Prophetess' (*CPW* iii. 170), first published in *Winter Words*.

Index